Concentrate your efforts on the study and discipline of Tae Kwon Do rather than just seeking maturity of technique.

The Complete Black Belt Hyung
Library of Congress Catalog Card Number: 88-092050
ISBN 0-929015-08-8

Copyright 1988 © by Master Hee Il Cho.
Published in the United States of America by Master Hee Il Cho.
All rights reserved. No part of this book may be reproduced in any manner
without written permission of
Master Hee Il Cho, 11304 1/2 Pico Blvd., Los Angeles, CA., 90064.

To My Mother:
    She is a person whose heart is bigger than a mountain,
        And wider than the ocean.
She has taught me to believe in myself,
    As strongly as she believes in herself.

Looking for perfection is like
    searching for fire with a torch.

It is for this reason that the ancients have said;
    to become perfect,
        return to it.

We are already perfect,
    and our "faults" are merely shades of that perfection.

If you really wish to become perfect,
    remember that you have never been anything less.

        *   *   *   *   *   *   *

* * * * * * *

Discard your ego. This is the true challenge of Tae Kwon Do.

Glory is temporary.
   Wisdom lasts forever.
      Train for a deeper understanding of
         Yourself.

About The Olympics...

Many martial artists have felt threatened by the inclusion of Tae Kwon Do as a demonstration sport in the 1988 Olympics games from Seoul. They have felt that, if Tae Kwon Do is not their style, then their style will somehow fall from grace. Such is not the case.

The mere fact that the world will be watching, interested, in this new event will bring honor not just to Tae Kwon Do, but to all schools of martial arts. All styles will benefit, because the personal achievement of Olympic competition transcends the competing sport. The Olympics are not a threat but a milestone, and I can only hope that Tae Kwon Do will become a permanent addition to the Olympic list of events.

I would like to congratulate all Olympic competitors, not only those who are participating in Tae Kwon Do. An Olympic athlete embodies the aims to achieve for all martial artists, and as such they deserve and have my utmost respect.

Dedication

DEDICATION

This book is dedicated to General Hong Hi Choi, President of the International Tae Kwon Do Federation, truly the "Father of Tae Kwon Do." It was General Choi who took the idea of several different Masters and created Tae Kwon Do. His love of the art transcends the unfortunate politics which, at present, surround it.

In the desert.

Deprived of food and water,
clothing and shelter,
family and friends.

Naked you are,
and alone.
What have you left?

Tae Kwon Do.

Table of Contents

BLACK BELT HYUNG

```
Copyright..................................................3-6
Dedication.................................................7-30
What is Tae Kwon Do........................................31-34
Master Hee Il Cho, A Biography.............................35-42
Philosophy of Master Hee Il Cho............................43-54
Master Hee Il Cho's Principles of Power....................55-62
Why Practice Patterns......................................63-66

Geum-Gahm.................................................67-80
Tae-Baek..................................................81-98
Pyeon-Won.................................................99-112
Sip-Jin...................................................113-130
Ji-Tae....................................................131-146
Cheon-Kwon................................................147-164
Han-Soo...................................................165-180
Il-Yeo....................................................181-194
First Aid Acupuncture Point...............................195-200

Master Cho's Photo Album..................................201-224
```

* * * * * * *

While training, your body and mind interact to create a harmony of motion and a relaxed mental state. During the performance of a hyung (pattern) many of your qualitites become apparent to the trained observer. Your dedication to the art, confidence, discipline, dilligence, strength – all of these are demonstrated by the act.

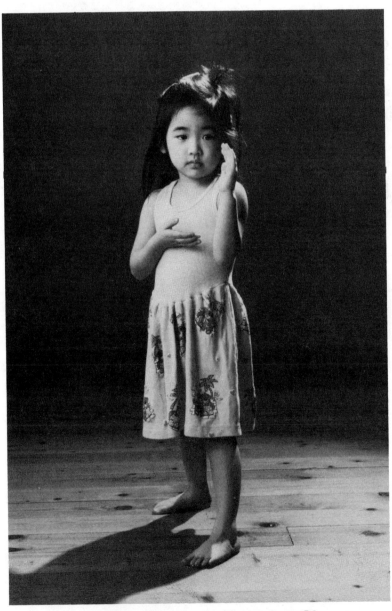

My daughter, Jasmine Cho.

Acknowledgements

While it is impossible to acknowledge everyone who has, in some way, contributed to the completeion of these publications, we must recognize those most directly involved.

Special recognition must be given to Jeff Schechter. Because of his involvement in nearly every phase of manuscript preparation, he may almost be considered the second author.

I would also like to single out the following people for their help in various ways during the writing of this book:

Kuy Ha Cho	David Goldner
In Kyu Cho	Eddie Ikuta
Steven O'Dell	Steven Krashen
Mario Veltri	Sung Woong Kim
David Carter	Marcello Real
Randy Goldstein	Jerry Isdale
Max Schachenmann	Kihyon Kim
Bobby Burns	

...and all the members of the Action International Martial Arts Association

My journey is one with which Tae Kwon Do
Has provided me great assistance.

Master Kuy Ha Cho, Vice President of the A.I.M.A.A.

CHO'S TAE KWON DO CENTER

June 8, 1988

Master Hee Il Cho
11304 1/2 Pico Blvd.
West Los Angeles, CA 90064

Master Cho:

I have just finished reviewing the final proofs of your new books. I am amazed at the amount of information and detail you have included in these volumes. I know that you have worked very hard for more than two years to complete these volumes and the end product shows the time that went into, and commitment to the quality of the books. You have completed what has to be the most thorough, authoritative and easy to understand reference books. When you look at the eleven books that you have completed, it is obvious that you have accomplished what no other martial artist has ever attempted before. You have left a record of your knowledge for all martial artists to benefit from in the future. You have accomplished this without promoting any specific martial arts style and have provided the instructor as well as the student an opportunity to learn and improve their skills.

I am very proud to be associated with these publications. I am confident that when these publications are available to the martial arts community, they will become the most authoritative training guides available.

Regards,

Kuy Ha Cho

TO MY WIFE, MIHYUN

I'd like to thank you, my beloved wife, for helping me a great deal with my life. Without your good spirits and support I could not have achieved all that I have. You are so patient, and your deep love for me has guided me to my success. I will always thank you for that.

To Mario Veltri:

    I would like to extend a special thanks to Mr. Mario Veltri, a person who has helped me a great deal with his kind support, intelligent advice and sincere concern. Even though my gratitude to him is always felt, it may not always be expressed. He is as good a friend as a person could hope to have. Thank you, Mario.

AIMAA Senior Students

Mr. Rick Kenton, Mr. Philip Ameris and Mr. Chris Scarborough - A.I.M.A.A.'s most senior students. Mr. Kenton and Mr. Scarborough have been students of Master Cho's since he first came to California, and Mr. Ameris has considered Master Cho his mentor since the early 1980's. These three excellent martial artists have almost fifty years of training between them!

I would like to express
  my heartfelt appreciation
    and thank you to

Jeff Schechter,
  without whose contribution
    and assistance

the creation of this book
  would never have been possible.

Hee U Cho

Where are you going?

Where did you come from?

Don't make the mistake of ego. At birth there are many paths, but only one which is yours.

Destiny makes victims of the weak. Step firmly along your path, your own, for it is not the trail's end but the trail itself which measures worth.

Don't announce to the world "I've finished!", but rather "I am!".

Remember, all paths lead back to the source.

TAE KWON-DO
KOREAN ART OF SELF DEFENCE

Chief Instructor
Master Hee IL Cho 8th Dan

Chairman
Mr D. Oliver, 7 Lime Avenue, Lillington, Leamington Spa CV32 7DE
Telephone (0926) 32154

Vice Chairman
Mr M. Dew, c/o Redfield Leisure Centre, 163 Church Road, Redfield, Bristol
Telephone (0272) 551046

Treasurer
Mr R. Sergiew, 585 Walsall Road, Great Wyrley, Walsall W56 6AE
Telephone (0922) 418844

National Secretary
Mr D. Atkins, 6 Avon Road, Whitnash, Leamington Spa CV31 2NJ
Telephone (0926) 36322

Tae Kwon Do Association of Great Britain Chairman, Mr. David Oliver

Master Hee Il Cho
Cho's Tae Kwon Do Centers
11304 1/2 Pico Boulevard
Los Angeles, California 90064

Dear Master Cho:

I am sorry we did not have more time to talk during your last visit to England. Hopefully this letter will convey the feelings of myself and members of the association I represent. Many years ago, you unselfishly accepted the responsibility of head instructor of this association. At that time this association was looking for innovative leadership as well as an individual who could provide a kind of high quality training and testing this association demands of its members. With your assistance, this association has now grown to more than 10,000 active members and with great pride looks to you as one of the primary forces in our success. Your international reputation and recognition as a martial artist instructor and author puts us in a unique position of being represented by an individual, who in our opinion, has no equal.

We look forward to the publication of your new books which we believe will be of great use to all of our members. On behalf of the Tae Kwon Do Association of Great Britain, let me extend my best wishes to you and your family.

Yours very truly,

Mr. David K. Oliver
Chairman
Tae Kwon Do Association
of Great Britain

All Ireland Tae Kwon·Do Association

NATIONAL SECRETARY,
17 VICAR STREET,
BARRACK STREET,
CORK,
IRELAND.

TEL: 021 964648

**All Ireland Tae Kwon Do Association Chairman,
Mr. Adrian Walsh**

Master Hee Il Cho
Cho's Tae Kwon Do Centers
11304 1/2 Pico Boulevard
Los Angeles, California 90064

Dear Master Cho:

I want to take this opportunity on behalf of the All Ireland Tae Kwon Do Association to thank you for your recent visit to Ireland in connection with our annual testing.

For more than six years, as our head instructor, our association has continued to grow and it is with great pride that we associate ourselves with you. It has been through your efforts, direction, and training that our association has grown into one of the largest in the nation. As our head instructor, we are extremely proud of the high reputation and standing you maintain in England, Ireland, and Europe in the martial arts community. Your dedication to the martial arts and training as well as the many books that you have published is a credit to you and all of those who associate with you.

Thank you again for your leadership and association with the All Ireland Tae Kwon Do Association. We look forward to your speedy return to Ireland.

Very truly yours,

Adrian Walsh
Chairman
All Ireland Tae Kwon Do
Association

To My Son, Jacob:

      I'm glad that you have never had to experience the same things which I did, growing up in Korea during a time of war. By the time I was your age, I was already feeling the burden of supporting my entire family; I'm happy that you haven't had to experience such problems.

      You must, however, understand a little hardship in order to appreciate all of the gifts you have been given. If you never see ugliness, how can you ever understand beauty? I want nothing bad for you, but you must work hard, always, in order that you can cherish life.

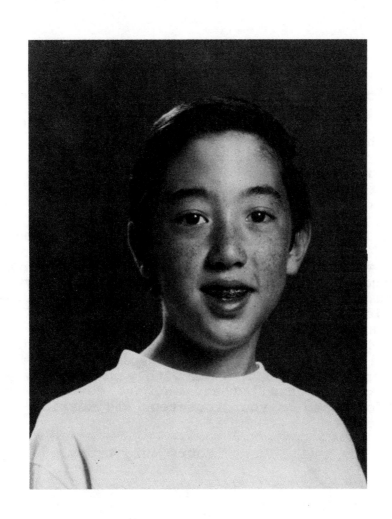

CHO'S TAE KWON DO CENTER

November 11, 1988

Hee Il Cho
11304 1/2 Pico Blvd.
West Los Angeles, Ca 90064

My dear brother:

After reviewing the proofs of the books, I can see now that it is in the final stages and when completed will be a major addition to the books you have already published.

I know from first hand experience that you have dedicated your life to the martial arts and these books are your legacy to those who wish to enrich themselves as you and the many thousand students who have trained under you have. For me, your inspiration, dedication and guidance have provided me with the foundation for my own personal development. Training with you these many years is a real honor as I know of no other individual who has dedicated his life to the martial arts as you have and whose dedication and inspiration is felt in each and every person who has trained with you. I know you realize how much I appreciate all that you have done for me. I look forward to following in your footsteps and working by your side in the future.

Yours very truly,

In Kyu Cho

Master In Kyu Cho, Chairman of the A.I.M.A.A.

MASTER CHO SHARES HIS KNOWLEDGE

WITH MARTIAL ARTISTS ALL AROUND THE WORLD.

What is Tae Kwon Do?

TAE - means kicking or smashing with the foot.
KWON - means punching with the fist.
DO - means the art or method of.

Combined, Tae Kwon Do means the art or method of kicking and punching, using the hands and feet. However, this is only the shallowest of meanings. Many people practice Tae Kwon Do as if it were written either **TAE** KWON DO or TAE **KWON** DO, focusing on purely the physical aspects of the art. Tae Kwon Do, however, should be written TAE KWON **DO**, because it is an art. There are levels and levels of understanding which makes it an art in the truest sense of the word; closer to painting it is than to exercise. TAE and KWON are merely the sport aspects of the discipline. They will not last. **DO**, on the other hand, will live beyond the failing of the physical aspects of the body.

The essence of all martial arts
Is founded on a union of
Mind and Body.

* * * * * * *

The common person looks and sees lumps of clay and pieces of coal. The martial artist looks and sees beautiful sculptures and magnificent diamonds. The martial artist has learned this from his training, where he was once clay and coal.

Training in the martial arts is like a jewel. It is merely a rough stone unless polished. If it is not polished, no one will know its inner beauty. Training is the same.

MASTER HEE IL CHO
A Biography

No other martial artist in the world has been invited to speak and demonstrate more that Master Hee Il Cho. An eighth-degree black belt in the Korean art of Taekwon Do, Master Cho is known throughout the world as one of the leading practitioners and innovators in the martial arts. His noteriety has led to more cover articles than any other martial artist in history.

Master Cho was born in Korea at the beginning of that country's bleakest hour. As a child he knew little other than the suffering and hunger brought about by war. The ability to survive was hard won. These childhood experiences helped mold his strong spirit.

Master Cho began studying Kang Soo Do at the age of ten after being severely beaten by a gang of youths at a local fair. He received his black belt at age thirteen, at which time he and his family moved to Inchon, near Seoul. Here, Master Cho began to study Taekwon Do, an art that would provide a lifetime of mental and physical development.

At the age of twenty one and already a fourth degree black belt, Master Cho was chosen to teach self-defence to the Korean Army. After his military service, Master Cho traveled to India and Germany where he taught servicemen the art of weaponless combat. Traveling with a demonstration team in 1969, Master Cho came to the United States and decided to stay.

After a brief time in Chicago, Master Cho settled and started teaching in South Bend , Indiana. Initially, times were hard but the indomitable spirit developed through the years of training allowed Master Cho to persevere. Eventually, He moved to Rhode Island and open a string of seven schools from 1972 through 1975.

Longing for warmth after a lifetime of bitterly remembered winters, Master Cho moved to Southern California in 1975. His school and reputation grew, and with it he recognized the need for a new organization; one based on the principles of Taekwon Do, but which would be for all martial arts diciplines. He founded the Action International Martial Arts Association which now enjoys worldwide membership of individuals and over a hundred schools. Through AIMAA, Master Cho hopes to reach all martial artists, regardless of the system they are studying and encourage in them them the true spirit of the martial arts.

Besides AIMAA, Master Cho is also the head instructor of both the England and Ireland Taekwon Do Associations. He visits and conducts seminars in Europe and other parts of the world on a regular basis.

As a tournament competitor, Master Cho has won more than twenty five championships around the world. He is the author of several successful martial arts books; "Man of Contrasts," a book of his techniques, philosophies and insights, "The Complete Taekwon Do Hung," a detailed three volume set which illustrates the various patterns practiced in Taekwon Do, "The Complete Martial Artist, Vols 1 and 2," a comprehensive exploration of the skills and training needed to for total mind, spirit and body fitness. To this impressive list of titles, Master Cho has recently completed five more books: "The Complete Master's Kick," "The Complete Master's Jumping Kick," "The Complete One Step and Three Step Sparring," "The Complete Tae Geuk Hyung of W.T.F," "The Complete Black Belt Hyung of W.T.F."

In addition to his written works, Master Cho has produced a series of over 31 instructional video tapes, the largest and most complete martial arts video library ever created by one person, including a video tape for Sybervision Inc. entitled "Defend Yourself."

While many masters of his caliber are content with writing and working behind a desk, Master Cho continues to work out and teach regularly at the AIMAA Headquarters, actively passing on his enthusiasm to his students.

As the title of Master Cho's first book so accurately states, Master Cho is a "Man of Contrasts." He has seen both devastating ugliness and inspirational beauty. He brings an understanding of both forces, light and dark to his growing legion of followers. He is what every student deserves; a cool breeze in the desert of false masters, an inspirational instructor and the complete martial artist.

> Life is full of changes
> Don't Resist
> Try Flowing

MASTER CHO SHARES HIS KNOWLEDGE

WITH MARTIAL ARTISTS ALL AROUND THE WORLD.

Does Kihap help?

Yes, it does. Morehouse and Miller, in their text, Physiology of Exercise, report that studies show that "maximum pulls against a tensometer were enhanced by 12.2% when the subject shouted loudly during a random final pull" (p. 56). Yelling makes you stronger, Morehouse and Miller suggest by reducing inhibitions.

What Research Says About Rest Pauses.

In Master Cho's classes, rest pauses are about 30 seconds long. I t turns out that 30 seconds may be optimal - longer rests would not be much better in restoring strength:

"Short, frequent rest pauses result in greater efficiency in muscular work than do prolonged, infrequent rests and are equally important in preventing loss of efficiency in skilled performance. Even after an elbow flexor muscle had been allowed to work to exhaustion, 69% of its strength was regained after 30 seconds. After a rest of 2.5 minutes only 13% more was regained, and after 7.5 minutes an additional 18% was regained. After a long pause of 42.5 minutes a total of 95% of its original strength was regained - only 26% more than after a 30 second rest." (From Morehouse and Miller, Physiology of Exercise, p. 54).

Does Rotating the Fist Help?

While some varieties of martial arts recommend rotating the fist while delivering a punch, very little seems to be gained. Physicist J.Walker calculated that the fist rotation adds about 0.4 joules of energy to a punch (one joule is the energy needed to lift one kilogram 10 centimeters). Since the energy contained in a good punch, according to Walker's calculations, is about 150 joules, Walker concludes that fist rotation makes a negligible contribution.

Walker, J. 1975. "Karate Strikes" American Journal of Physics 43:845-849

Three Workouts Per Week?

Master Cho requires three workouts a week. According to research, three workouts per week may be just about right. Studies show that three workouts per week produces a significantly better conditioning effect than two or one workouts. More than three workouts means little or no additional gain, however. Studies cited by Morehouse and Miller (1976) show that five workouts per week result in only a 3.5% increase in aerobic power when compared with three workouts, and that "cardiovascular fitness is retained nearly as effectively by three sessions per week as by four sessions per week." (p. 235) Other studies (Crews and Roberts, 1976) show no difference between three and five days per week. Morehouse and Miller also point out, however, that one or two sessions per week will give some improvement if training is intensive: "The notion that one workout per week is worse than none at all is invalid." (p. 235)

References:

Crews, T. and Roberts J. 1976. "Effect of Interaction of Frequency and Intensity of Training", Research Quarterly

Morehouse, L. and Miller, A. 1976. Physiology of Exercise, Saint Louis: Mosby. Seventh Edition.

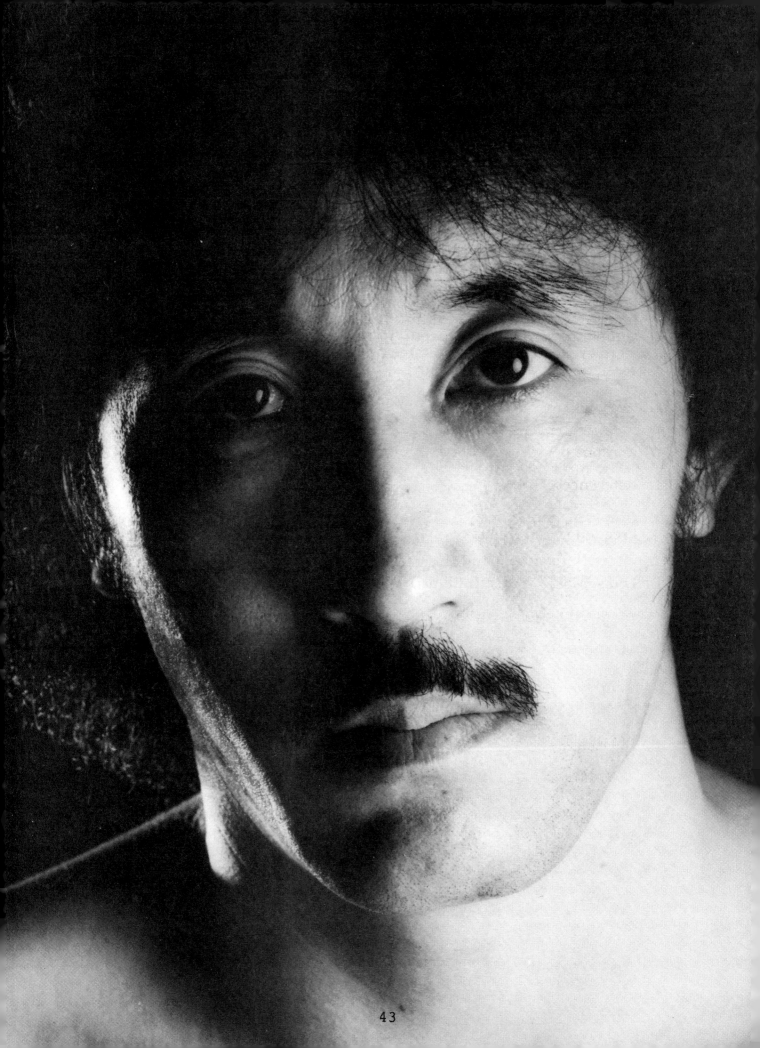

Philosophy of Master Hee Il Cho

In the days following World War II, Korea was a country looking for an identity, searching aimlessly for its soul.

More than 30 years of Japanese occupation had destroyed the country's culture and all but buried one of its most important resources -- martial arts. Oh, there were scores of young martial artists looking for fights, thinking they were the toughest kid on the block. And I was one of them. But the foundation of the Korean arts, its philosophy, had disappeared with the country's independence. Three decades of imposed rule had robbed Korea of most of its true masters. Gone were most of the old-world instructors who considered martial arts to be an equal combination of spirit and techniques. Mastering one without learning the other was like having a body, but no mind, they believed.

Still, in those early days we didn't know any better. No one talked about philosophy; only fighting. It wasn't how disciplined you were, but who you could beat. We had struggled to survive for so long, we forgot when the war was over that so was our conflict. Instead, the emphasis was still on surviving, taking care of yourself before anyone else. Back then martial arts catered to the street people, those not so well-educated. There were a few exceptions, such as some students living and training in the mountain monasteries, but I didn't believe studying with old masters would teach me how to fight. As with most of us, I believed the only way you could learn how to fight was to experience the thrill of combat.

I guess you could say we had a philosophy, but I know now it was not the right philosophy. When I started practicing, the master was the God image. I believed he could blink and eye and kill anybody. Or if he worked out, he would be so fast no one could see him. His speed was that mysterious. I seldom saw him, just a lot of his black belt students teaching us. He gave a little speech before testing and then he was gone.

As far as the martial artists, they hated each other. They would say "We are the best, we are the strongest" and we would fight at different street corners, different dojo, almost like a Bruce Lee movie. I believed my master was the best. I showed him true loyalty. It was almost as if I was brainwashed. I couldn't see what was good or evil. And I believed my style was the best. I was willing to die to prove it. But as I found out later, if the frog stays in a little pond, he thinks he knows the world. But when he gets to the ocean, he is lost.

That's exactly how I felt when I came to the United States in 1969. I was lacking a philosophy, a true meaning for studying my discipline, but I didn't know it. I came here thinking I was the toughest, meanest fighter that ever lived. And that my style, Taekwon Do, was second to none. I wanted to prove that, to challenge every one and anything that crossed my path. I did, and I got the shock of my life. As time went by I competed and lost a couple of matches in point tournaments. I couldn't believe it. I was using my jumping spinning kicks and the Japanese stylists would not even move. They would just stand there, throw a reverse punch to my ribs and score.
discipline, humility, ego, concentration and focus, fighting, and training. These are the values I continually impart to my students and these are the values I will share with you.

I realized that at the age of 27, I would have to develop my own philosophy. Hundreds of years ago, philosophy was the foundation upon which all form and technique were built. Martial artists searched for the meaning in their lives and tried to instill order. From this order came form and from form came technique. Philosophy is not just religion, as in Buddhism or Taoism, but in using its practical applications in our daily lives. Masters in ancient Korea had the right idea, but somehow the principles of martial arts philosophy got lost in wanting to be the best, the strongest or the fastest. I remember someone once suggesting to me that sooner or later I would have to give up being a performing martial artist and start being a teacher. At the time I maintained I would still be doing demonstrations when I was 70 years of age. I'd still do jumping spinning kicks off the ceiling, I promised. Well now I'm approaching 50 and would you believe it, I can't do it! When I was 30 I thought masters weren't actively teaching and demonstrating because they were phonies, frauds. They didn't do it because they couldn't do it. I never had respect for my seniors because they never did anything. I never saw one do a demonstration, so how could they be in shape? I realized there was more to being a black belt, more to being a good teacher than wiping up the floor with another fighter or tickling the chandelier with a kick. I learned you must first develop a philosophy, a guiding light for both you and your students to follow through the rigors of training in one of life's most demanding disciplines.

Being a good martial arts student involves time, dedication and motivation, as well as a rock solid philosophy that will help you through the rough times. The components of that philosophy are: flexibility, timing,

Flexibility

You have to develop a philosophy of being flexible, of being adaptable to change, to progress in the martial arts. This means you have to be open to new ideas as well as training principles. I realized when I came to this country that my style was not the only good style around. I noticed after losing on several occasions that Taekwon Do was not the lone superior style, although that has not prevented it from becoming the most popular martial arts style in the world.

In Korea, since most people studied Taekwon Do, kicks were prevalent and hand techniques were seldom used. But we never faced fighters from other styles. At a tournament soon after I came here, I saw most of the martial artists win by using the reverse punch or the ridge hand. So I adopted that. I opened my mind. After all, what good are high or flashy kicks if they don't work in a practical fighting situation?

Every athlete is getting better in the United States because they are opening their minds to new theories. What coaches and trainers do not understand, they study. They discover that the body may produce more if trained a certain way, or an athlete may execute a technique better if positioned at a different angle. I kept entering tournaments here because I wanted to learn more about something I didn't know. If you have a narrow mind, very still, then you won't grasp other styles or grasp the philosophy behind the techniques. For example, when Taekwon Do fighters face Shotokan stylists, they must use more hand skills. Subsequently, Taekwon Doists become better fighters with their hands. The more knowledge you have, the better off you are.

Also, when your attitude is flexible, you can adapt more things more quickly into your style. You can understand why certain techniques work a certain way, and why you might have to discard a favorite move in favor of one that might be more effective.

To increase your effectiveness, you must be physically flexible. Your kicks look better and your techniques are easier to execute. If your attitude is flexible, you can push yourself towards physical flexibility. As time and age come, you must understand your physical flexibility will decrease. But if your attitude is strong, yet open to change, your mind will grow as it absorbs more. You get better and better. You become more flexible, and better off in a martial arts sense.

Timing

A fighter whose timing is off just one half second can end up on the wrong side of a punch or kick. Timing is very important in martial arts training or any field of endeavor. The philosophy of timing deals with organizing your life in such a manner that it is always working in your favor. Being there at the right time and at the right place with the right execution will make you a winner most of the time.

Life is full of examples of good and bad timing. Sometimes, through no fault of your own, your may be at the wrong place at the wrong time. Say for instance you're involved in an accident. But there are times when better timing could produce a happy ending. If you have a big business meeting and you're a half hour late or you miss your flight, it could cost you your livelihood. You have to train your mind to use good timing and you can use that in your martial arts endeavors.

Adjusting your timing is not nearly as difficult as it appears. You just have to constantly be thinking about what you're doing. If you go to church and merely listen, you're not understanding what is being said. If you concentrate on the preacher's words, and try to live your life accordingly, then you're letting timing work for your. You should also think about developing that skill.

And that brings us back to martial arts. Timing is one of the martial artist's greatest allies. I know I sometimes have trouble with my timing. But I know that, and I continually work towards improving that deficiency. The first time you try, you may fail. If you continue to work, you'll find you get better. That's like punching 10 times. If it doesn't work, try 20 times. And if that doesn't work, try 2,000 times. It's the same thing in life. Some people actually reach their goals and others fall by the wayside. The people who have actually made it have worked on improving their timing. When you have a problem with timing, you must work to eliminate it.

Discipline

I am much more publicized than most of the masters around the country or the world. But many think the 11 books I've written and the 30 video tapes I've done somehow came after one day's work. However, I worked weekends, 12-hour days. Whenever I had a free moment. I knew what I wanted and I was determined to get it. I was willing to spend the time. This is called discipline.

Training is difficult for many people who join my school. It's after work, you're tired, you might like to sit in front of the tv and drink a beer. It's very inviting. But if you decide to push yourself a little more now, you'll be happier later in life. As a more disciplined person, you will have brought order into your work and personal life.

What makes a disciplined martial artist? That's hard to say, but in many cases it starts with the instructor. If he teaches you the right way with the right philosophy, he will create in you a drive to become better. Hopefully, you'll take care of the rest. Unfortunately, there are many unqualified instructors out there who think total training begins and ends with sparring. The undisciplined martial artist will be taught that philosophy means nothing, that being competitive is the path to take. Martial arts is not just for competition; it is for realizing your limitations and then using your discipline to wipe away those limitations. If you look at a brown belt and say , "He's better than me," well, he may be younger stronger and faster. Instead of looking at someone else, look at what you've accomplished. Now you have discipline. You've been training for a long time and you have courage.

Ego

I have many students and their biggest problem is to bow when they enter the dojo. They have trouble saying "Yes sir," and "No sir," to people they don't know or respect. People having the most problems are degreed personnel such as doctors and lawyers. They have worked hard to achieve a position and are not very willing to bow to someone else. The problem is one of ego.

But if they don't give up and keep training, they will reconstruct their whole attitude and discover they lacked confidence when they came in. When your whole attitude changes, you have true self-confidence and have lost your ego. Then you can respect yourself and easily say, "Yes sir," "No sir." If you don't respect yourself, you cannot respect anybody else. If a person can bow and realize he doesn't know something, or that he knows less that the instructor, he can be a great asset to the martial arts. And the martial arts can be a great asset to him.

Mind and Body

When your mind and body are harmonized, you will be much calmer. You won't be nervous and you won't suffer physically. If your mind and body can be fused as one, you'll be much happier because you'll be understanding, accepting.

As with any phase of life, you'll suffer if your mind is one place and your body somewhere else. An instructor cannot just teach the physical, or just teach the spiritual. There's no way you can accentuate body over mind. If you take away the brain, you are paralyzed; you no longer function. That means if you take out the brain and place it on the table, the brain itself will be useless.

The brain and the body are one, and you try to harmonize the body and mind. Sometimes it can be very difficult, especially during martial arts training. There's so much concentration during forms practice, your mind and body must function together. When sparring, if these two entities are a single unit, you will be difficult to hit. If not, you can get nailed by a slow moving truck.

Don't get me wrong. As with most martial arts training, learning to harmonize the body and the mind takes time. It is especially difficult to teach children. Their minds and bodies are not working together. They're young and their attention span is limited.

Most people who join a karate class are in their early 20's. Unfortunately, their minds have been set. It's very difficult to change their characters. The problems they had while growing up are still with them. They won't change in two months or two years. Maybe 10 years. But if they're children, we can bring mind and body together in two years or less.

Mind and body harmonization is most important in the execution of forms. If the master is trying to teach you a 68-step form, and your mind and body are not together, you'll never memorize the steps. But if you're focusing , flowing, allowing your mind and body to become one, then sooner or later you're no longer thinking , just doing. You will do it automatically.

Fighting

Gaining self-confidence is the most important aspect in our lives. However, many people go through life lacking confidence. You can achieve an academic-type confidence by graduating from college or a skill-type confidence from learning a trade. But in the martial arts, physical confidence can only be gained by learning how to fight and knowing how to take care of yourself in a real situation.

Many martial arts schools won't emphasize sparring. Some business people don't want to be hit hard in the face, while other instructors fear the possibility of lawsuits brought about by injury. But if you're not going to emphasize sparring, you must teach them self-confidence and self-control, but how can you expect true confidence without an emphasis on sparring ? You won't know what a true martial art is and what it can offer you.

Fighting is imperative in the martial arts. Without fighting, you're not understanding total and complete martial arts, because until you get physically hit by someone, you won't know if something works. The instructor must bring his student along slowly, so he can allow his confidence level to grow. And his confidence can grow only by getting as close as possible to real physical training. If all you do is forms, touch hands, shadowboxing and working out alone, then you go into the ring and get hit, you'll' be in trouble because you won't know how to react.

Training

You can eat breakfast, lunch and dinner in one sitting and then not eat for the rest of the day. Or you could try to eat a month's worth of meals in just one week. Your stomach couldn't take the pace and you would get sick. The same holds true for your training regimen. If I haven't worked out for a week, my workouts are different than if I had bee working out for that week. When I take a vacation, I've found I've lost everything when I return to the dojo. My muscles hurt, my reactions are slower.

Your philosophy of training should be the same as breathing. You need to do it every day to survive. To stay in shape, to hone your skills, you need to train on a regular basis.

Many people get disillusioned with training. At first the gains are considerable., But after a while, as your skills become sharper, the improvements are barely noticeable. And it's easier to get frustrated. What you have to consider is what you'll look and feel like if you stop.

This goes back to the philosophy on discipline. Even when you feel like quitting, you must reach back and gather the strength to continue. You must have faith in your routine and your instructor. You have to say to yourself that this is a necessary part of my life.

If you can get through these low periods, you'll soon find you can't go without training. You know if you stop your body will become flabby and you'll lose pride in yourself. You won't want to throw your body in a junkheap.

Conclusion

In this day and age, it is rare to find an instructor who emphasizes philosophy as much as physical technique or training. For most instructors today, the most important thing is to find a good location and develop a business. Martial arts teachers have become businessmen. As such, the spiritual aspect may become lost in their drive for success.

In the same vein, students are not as apt to request teaching in the philosophical side of martial arts. For the two or three hours they spend at the dojo, they may just want to exercise the body. It is virtually impossible in that small time period to explain the roots of the discipline. Most practitioners cannot be expected to desire the things their ancestors did in ancient Korea.

But for those few who want more from their martial art than self-defense techniques and a well-built frame, there should be instructors who are willing to provide the total foundation.

The philosophies outlined in the preceding pages are merely a map to follow during your martial arts training. No one said it would always be easy. As with anything worthwhile in life, martial arts takes time, dedication discipline, a will to excel and a willingness to accept and respect those more talented than you.

Most of all, the martial arts are a microcosm of life. They have philosophies that work as well outside the dojo as when you're training. If you concentrate on the virtues of flexibility, fighting and training, and allow them to spill over into your daily life, you will be happier and more successful in anything you do.

Master Cho's Principles of Power

MASTER CHO'S PRINCIPLES OF POWER

There is a real danger in any traditional system of learning, be it a physical system, an intellectual system or a spiritual system, and that danger is that traditional systems tend to be closed systems, allowing no room for questions or modifications. They are taught by people who do not expect to be challenged, just as they did not challenge their teachers who did not challenge *their* teachers. It is exactly these types of systems which Master Hee Il Cho has fought against in his martial arts training methods.

Not that there is anything wrong with traditions and traditional ways of training, mind you. Master Cho is the first to incorporate these into his classes. However, to ignore a broader, more enlightened view of the martial arts is to ignore what Master Cho calls the Principles of Power. And because the Principles of Power are a fusion of tradition and science, one cannot be locked into any mind set and still follow Master Cho's teachings.

In order to fully understand Master Cho's Principles of Power, one must first accept one of Master Cho's main beliefs; that a person is composed of three "selves" - a physical self, an intellectual self, and a spiritual self; all meant to work together to create a sense of unity, of completeness. To support this idea, picture someone reading a very moving passage from a book. Their "physical" self enables the person to open the book and see the pages, their "intellectual" self enables them to read and understand the words on the pages, and their "spiritual" self is moved by what those words mean. When a person is operating at peak ability, all three "selves" are being nurtured and used, and denying one "self" in favor of another is as wrong as having three children and not taking care of all of them equally. Real Power, therefore, is to Master Cho not just physical, but intellectual and spiritual as well.

After accepting the idea of the three "selves", the Principles of Power are quite easy to understand; as people, we have certain limitations based on our height, weight, education and backgrounds, however when you refine these through Tae Kwon Do training, you can achieve "completeness", not just as a martial artist but as a person.

Even the Principles of Power's most basic aspect, that physical well-being has a positive effect on intellectual abilities and emotional stability, has been well documented in recent years by doctors and researchers. However, as reasonable as Master Cho's philosophy sounds, it still flies in the face of a stodgy establishment and older thinking. Master Cho once received a letter from a martial artist and research scientist whose Director of Research had insisted that the scientist stop teaching Tae Kwon Do during his leisure hours because the time spent on Tae Kwon Do could be spent on more scientific pursuits.

"This is very sad." commented Master Cho. "The Director doesn't realize the connection between the physical well-being of a person and that person's mental abilities." Very true, for what the Director is actually doing by insisting that the scientist stop training is insisting that the scientist lose a certain amount of his mental quickness, clearly something that the Director wouldn't want to happen.

Master Cho is quick to point out that this is just one instance out of many such stories that he is aware of - the tough instructors who are all fight and no mind; the religiously zealous who turn their back on scientific education - these are all examples of depriving one "self" in favor of another; to be a whole person you must train the whole person.

Over the last 40 years during which Master Cho has been training and learning, he has defined a system of training, and indeed living, which seeks to combine the "selves" and create maximum power for each. Some of his ideas are immediately clear sounding and understandable, while others contradict some things which people have thought for years. All ideas however, are clearly rooted in science and immutable physical laws.

Perhaps Master Cho's most glaring innovations have come in the pursuit of the physical Principles of Power. We have all seen the classic shot of a person performing a jumping side kick; one leg straight out in side kick position with the other leg tucked underneath the person's body. Well, you won't see Master Cho ever teaching this kick in this manner. Why not?

"Because it doesn't make sense to kick that way!" is Master Cho's frank reply. "It isn't scientific and it ignores some basic scientific concepts."

Pictures of Master Cho performing this and similar kicks line the walls of his studio, and in every picture you can see Master Cho's way of kicking - the kicking leg extended and the other leg jutting out in the opposite direction. "This," according to Master Cho "is the only sensible way of throwing this type of kick."

Master Cho creates a very effective argument for kicking in this manner, especially when witnessing the power which he is able to generate as he kicks the hanging bag.

"The traditional way of tucking your leg came about for two reasons." Master Cho says. "First, it was felt that you should protect your groin when jumping, and second because it looked more dramatic, but neither is reason enough to sacrifice the power which could be there if it were thrown in a more scientific manner."

Science has always been Master Cho's greatest ally, and he has incorporated his understanding of it into his theories of punching and blocking as well as kicking, often debunking those martial artists who claim to have achieved super-human powers and mystical "death touches."

"There is no mystery to the martial arts." Master Cho says. "If you want to kick harder, than you have to understand the Principles of Power. If you want to punch harder you have to understand the Principles of Power."

But what about that jutting opposite leg?

"Here's some science." Master Cho says during a pause in his punishment of the hanging bag. "Science says that force is the relationship between how much something weighs and how fast it is moving, so if you want to kick stronger, a good way would be for you to make your leg heavier and kick faster, right?"

This seemed reasonable, but how do you change the weight of your leg? "You can't change how much your leg actually weighs, but you change how much it *seems* to weigh by putting more body weight into the kick. That's why those martial artists who just flick out their legs may have fast kicks, but they hit without any real power." Master Cho then demonstrated what he meant with a single kick to the bag, stepping into the technique and leaning his weight into his kicking leg to make his leg an extension of his body weight. The bag reeled from the blow.

"Okay, so you make the kick seem heavier by using your body weight, and then by torquing your waist you speed the kick up. To increase the torquing action, you must extend your opposite leg. It's the difference between swinging a small stick and swinging a baseball bat. The baseball bat helps to create greater torque." Again Master Cho demonstrated with equal effect. Clearly, he is a man who has spent a lot of time not just performing the martial arts, but thinking about the martial arts as well.

"Here's some more science...every action has an equal and opposite reaction, right? The leg shooting out in the opposite direction satisfies this Principle of Power as well. Why should a Tae Kwon Do kick be excused from these truths?"

It's hard to argue with a person who makes his point so clearly, and then backs it up with action.

"Punches and blocks follow the same Principles of Power as kicks. Use your body weight to increase the weight of the technique, use the torqing action of your waist to increase the speed, and you have now made the technique as strong as you are able to based on your natural abilities."

Once again Master Cho backs up this theory with an effective demonstration. First he punches, showing how by pushing in with the punching hand's shoulder you increase the weight of the punch and by turning your opposite shoulder away from the punch you also increase the speed, maximizing the force of the blow.

Next, Master Cho blocks, torquing his waist to generate speed and driving his weight into the blocking technique. For all the power generated, neither the blocks nor the punches appear sloppy or stiff; they flow with an incredible ease inspite of their great strength.

Any martial artist who has achieved Master Cho's level of physical excellence would probably be content, but to be content based on his physical achievements does not sit well at all with Master Cho because it represents only one of his "selves". What Master Cho's Principles of Power have done for him physically, they have also done for him mentally and spiritually as well.

Besides being one of the best, Master Cho has an intellectual determination to help those who want to learn what he has learned, and to this end he has created the most impressive library of video training aids ever created for the martial arts by a single person. Over 30 tapes currently exist in Master Cho's library, and these tapes are the continuing expansion and reporting of Master Cho's discoveries about the martial arts in general and Tae Kwon Do in particular, as well as being one of the most popular series of tapes on the martial arts available worldwide.

In addition to this achievement, Master Cho is now planning the construction of a multi-million dollar training facility, the largest martial arts and fitness complex in the United States. Besides training in Tae Kwon Do, there will be full weight training equipment, saunas and spas, massage rooms, aerobic counselors and physical therapists, accupuncturists, video training rooms and even dormitories where students can stay inexpensively in order to train with Master Cho personally. This still un-named center has been one of Master Cho's dreams, and he has pursued it through obstacles and set-backs for the past few years with a resolve and determination which hasn't flagged. If anything indicates Master Cho's ideas about the mental Principles of Power, then the concept of bringing this training facility to life certainly does.

Master Cho's spiritual Principles of Power were forged initially out of the hardships that befell him and his family during the Korean War, and then further formed through his training in Tae Kwon Do and his adventures in the United States, where he arrived one winter's night with $10.00 in his pocket and went on to take the country by storm.

"I certainly don't think everyone should go through what I went through." Master Cho says. "But a little adversity is good for a person's character. Everyone can handle the good things in life; it is the unfortunate things that happen to us sometimes which really teach us about ourselves and life."

To satisfy the need for achieving a spiritual Principle of Power, Master Cho believes that Tae Kwon Do is the best way in a controlled enviornment.

"Tae Kwon Do is the most physically demanding of the martial arts," he points out. "and because of this it is also the most spiritual."

How's that again? Because it's the most physical it's also the most spiritual?

"Because it is the most demanding," Master Cho explains. "it teaches you rather quickly what your physical limitations are. In the hands of an enlightened student, this information makes them wonder what their mental and spiritual limitations are as well, because you cannot have the knowledge of one without the understanding that the other two also exist. It is exactly this studying of yourself that is needed to advance yourself spiritually. That's why I've always felt that Tae Kwon Do was one of the best things a person could do for themselves. Done properly, it helps to educate a person about their physical, mental and spiritual selves. I don't know of any one activity that does this as effectively."

Again, Master Cho has made a convincing argument for his Principles of Power - physical, intellectual and spiritual - though to think of them seperately is misguided. As Master Cho points out, a person who does so risks not being "complete," and as Master Cho has shown his students over and over again, being a complete martial artist as well as a complete human being is the best place to be.

If your mind is confused,
You will not be able to see yourself.

WHY PRACTICE PATTERNS?

Practically every style or system of the martial arts has patterns or forms; prearranged series of movements that blend into a martial arts dance. Japanese styles call them "kata," Korean styles call them "hyung" and "poomse."

The idea behind the patterns seems simple enough; design a set of movements for students to practice at each belt level, starting more simply and increasing the difficulty as the student progresses. To the layperson, learning patterns might seem like a reasonable way of teaching various techniques and nothing else. While the learning of techniques is a crucial part of learning the martial arts, it is neither the most important nor is it the only reason why patterns are taught.

The human being is composed of three selves; the physical, the intellectual and the spiritual. The goal of training in the martial arts is to gain mastery of all three of these components. This is why we study patterns.

Obviously, performing a pattern requires physical control because all techniques must be performed strongly and precisely. This is why the beginning student is encouraged to take his or her time in achieving, being made to place a great emphasis on understanding how the body moves and relates to the space surrounding him or her. The physicality of the pattern teaches students about their bodies.

Because the pattern remains constant and the movements must be learned, the pattern also incorporates the intellectual side of the student. Even the seemingly easy task of learning the movements of the patterns becomes magnified in difficulty as the student advances in ability and belt level and must therefore remember more patterns, being careful not to confuse the elements of one with another. The study of patterns serves to teach the student how to focus mentally, keeping a clear mind and zeroing in on the task at hand.

The patterns also have a spiritual side to them, often coming from the meaning and the principles of the patterns as detailed by their creators. It is not unusual for a pattern to have either a religious or historical meaning which serves to illustrate qualities which the student should strive for in his or her daily life. For this reason, whenever a student is required to learn a pattern, he or she is also required to know its meaning.

THE PHILOSOPHY OF THE TAE-GEUK PATTERNS

Literally translated, "tae" means "bigness" and "geuk" mean eternity. Combined, tae-geuk is taken to mean the "great eternity." There are no elements outside of the "great eternity," and therefore the principles behind the tae-geuk patterns are all-inclusive and pervasive.

The first eight patterns of the tae-geuk series derive their meanings from the basic tenents of one of the Orient's oldests philosophical works - the Book of Changes, also called the "I Ching" by the Chinese and "Jooyeok" by the Koreans. At once a major religious work as well as an oracle used to disclose future events, the Book of Changes was based on the understanding of the interchange between the powers of opposites; clasically "yin" and "yang" ("um" and "yang" in Korean).

"Yin" is the ultimate creative power, unbridled in its

ability, while "yang" is the ultimate receptive power, taking in and nourishing all. The powers of "yin" and "yang" are identified by eight subsequent manifestations of this creative/receptive concept; Keon which is pure "yin" and represents the universe, Tae which represents lasting joy, Ri which represents fire and light, Jun with represents thunder, Seon which represents wind, Gam which represents water, Gan which represents the calm mountain, and Gon which represents the receptive earth and which is a concept that is totally "yang." These eight symbols are arranged in a circle across from their opposite and complementary symbol to demonstrate the continuity of nature; the universe (heaven) is across from the earth (keon/gon), joy is opposite from calm (tae/gan), fire is across from water (ri/gam), and thunder (noise without substance) is across from wind (substance without noise - jin/seon).

The second eight patterns of the tae-geuk series start with Koryo pattern which is included in this volume. These patterns represent little lessons in Korean history which help to illustrate a point about either human nature or character. the Koryo pattern, for example, has at its heart the concept of cultivating strong convictions and an unyielding spirit; valuable tools not just for the martial artist but for everyone.

To understand the subtlety and beauty of learning patterns, a student must labor for years, forever refining and cleaning technique as well as meditating deeply on meaning. By embracing the tae-geuk patterns and their meanings, it is hoped that serious students of the martial arts can better themselves physically, intellectually and spiritually.

GEUM-GAHG

GEUNM-GANG HYUNG

Mt. Geunm-Gang is located in central Korea and is famous for the majesty of its bearing as well as its inexpressible beauty. Composed of more than twelve thousand peaks, Geunm-Gang is only one name out of four which the mountain has to represent the four seasons.

So beautiful that it is referred to as "the Shangri-La of Korea," Mt. Geunm-Gang was considered an ideal place for those people who were seeking seclusion to pursue religious ideals and to meditate.

GEUNM-GANG HYUNG, like its namesake, literally means "hardness"; the basis for impregnable power combined with strong wisdom and virtue.

GEUNM-GANG HYUNG READY POSITION.

1a. Crossing the arms at the elbows, shift your weight onto your right foot and step forward with the left foot.

1b. Assume a left forward stance while executing a low section wedging block with both arms.

3b. Assume a left forward stance while simultaneously executing a left palm heel strike to face level.

4a. Bringing your right hand back to your waist, shift your balance onto your left foot, stepping forward with your right foot.

4b. Assume a right forward stance while simultaneously executing a right palm heel strike to face level.

69

2a. Bringing your right hand back to your waist, shift your balance onto your left foot, stepping forward with your right foot.

2b. Assume a right forward stance while simultaneously executing a right palm heel strike to face level.

3a. Bringing your left hand back to your waist, shift your balance onto your right foot, stepping forward with your left foot.

5a. Shift your balance onto your left foot and bring both arms 90 degrees to your sides while stepping backwards with your right foot.

5b. Assume a right back stance while executing an inward knifehand strike with the left hand.

6a. Shift your balance onto your right foot and bring both arms 90 degrees to your sides while stepping backwards with your left foot.

6b. Assume a left back stance while executing an inward knifehand strike with the right hand.

7a. Shift your balance onto your left foot and bring both arms 90 degrees to your sides while stepping backwards with your right foot.

7b. Assume a right back stance while executing an inward knifehand strike with the left hand.

9b. Assume a riding horse stance while simultaneously executing a circular punch with your right hand.

10a, b. Shift your weight onto your left foot and step to your left a full 180 degrees, pivoting on the ball of your left foot.

8a. Bringing both arms to in front of your chest, cross both arms and shift your balance onto your right foot, raising your left foot off the ground and turning your body 90 degrees to your left side.

8b. Assuming a crane stance, execute a high section block with your right hand while simultaneously executing a low section block with your left hand.

9a. Bringing both arms to your sides, shift your balance forward, bringing your left foot down.

10c,d. Continue this turning motion, stepping to your left another 180 degrees. Assume a riding horse stance while executing another circular punch with your left arm.

11a. Shifting your balance onto your left foot, raise your right leg high and to the outside.

72

11b. Execute an outside to inside crescent kick with the right leg, turning your body 90 degrees counter-clockwise.

11c, d. Crossing your arms in front of your body, bring your right foot down in a riding horse stance while simultaneously executing a "W" shaped block with both arms. KI-HAP!

13b. Continuing slowly, execute a double low section block while assuming a ready stance.

14a. Shifting balance onto your right foot, raise your left leg high and to the outside.

14b. Execute an outside to inside crescent kick with the left leg, turning your body 180 degrees clockwise.

12a. Shift your weight onto your right foot, turning 180 degrees clockwise on the ball of the right foot.

12b. Crossing both arms in front of your body, assume a riding horse stance while executing a wedging block with both arms.

13a. Slowly, straighten up, pulling your left foot towards your right while crossing both arms in front of your upper body.

14c, d. Crossing your arms in front of your body, bring your left foot down in a riding horse stance while simultaneously executing a "W" shaped block with both arms.

15a. Bringing both arms to in front of your chest, shift your balance onto your left foot, raising your right foot off the ground and turning your body 90 degrees to your right side.

15b. Assuming a crane stance, execute a high section block with your left hand while simultaneously executing a low section block with your right hand.

16a. Bringing both arms to your sides, shift your balance forward, bringing your right foot down.

16b. Assume a riding horse stance while simultaneously executing a circular punch with your left hand.

17a, b. Shift your weight onto your right foot and step to your right a full 180 degrees, pivoting on the ball of your right foot.

18a. Shifting your balance onto your right foot, raise your left leg high and to the outside.

18b. Execute an outside to inside crescent kick with the left leg, turning your body 90 degrees clockwise.

17c,d. Continue this turning motion, stepping to your right another 180 degrees. Assume a riding horse stance while executing another circular punch with your left arm.

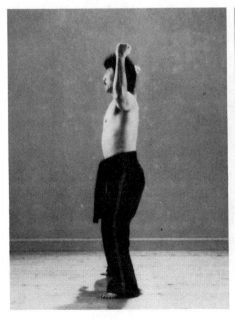  

18c, d. Crossing your arms in front of your body, bring your right foot down in a riding horse stance while simultaneously executing a "W" shaped block with both arms. KI-HAP!

19a. Shift your weight onto your left foot, turning 180 degrees counter-clockwise on the ball of the left foot.

19b. Crossing both arms in front of your body, assume a riding horse stance while executing a wedging block with both arms.

20a. Slowly, straighten up, pulling your right foot towards your left while crossing both arms in front of your upper body.

20b. Continuing slowly, execute a double low section block while assuming a ready stance.

21a. Shifting balance onto your left foot, raise your right leg high and to the outside.

22a. Bringing both arms to in front of your chest, shift your balance onto your right foot, raising your left foot off the ground and turning your body 90 degrees to your left side.

22b. Assuming a crane stance, execute a high section block with your right hand while simultaneously executing a low section block with your left hand.

23a. Bringing both arms to your sides, shift your balance forward, bringing your left foot down.

77

21b. Execute an outside to inside crescent kick with the right leg, turning your body 180 degrees counter-clockwise.

21c, d. Crossing your arms in front of your body, bring your right foot down in a riding horse stance while simultaneously executing a "W" shaped block with both arms.

23b. Assume a riding horse stance while simultaneously executing a circular punch with your right hand.

24a, b. Shift your weight onto your left foot and step to your left a full 180 degrees, pivoting on the ball of your left foot.

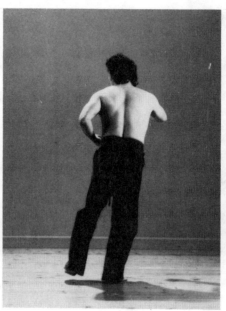

24c,d. Continue this turning motion, stepping to your left another 180 degrees. Assume a riding horse stance while executing another circular punch with your right arm.

25a, b. Shifting your balance onto your right foot, bring your left foot and hands back to the ready position.

TAE-BAEK

TAE-BAEK HYUNG

The story of TAE-BAEK was introduced in the myth of Dan Gun, the legendary founder of Korea. TAE-BAEK is a beautiful mountain which is thought to embody the spirit of the sun due to the striking colors of its trees each autumn.

Even though its name was changed to Baek-Du, TAE-BAEK still exists at the border beteen Korea and China. It is felt that the mountain's purpose is to enlighten people on the profound philosophy of the continuity of the past, present and future.

TAE-BAEK HYUNG is represented by the diagram (工) which represents the union of heaven, earth and man. The upper part of the diagram (「工」) means heaven, the middle (「工」) represents man and the bottom of the diagram (「工」) signifies the earth.

The essence of TAE-BAEK HYUNG is to apply the sanctified spirit of TAE-BAEK to the mind and body, making one quick in action.

TAE-BAEK HYUNG
READY POSITION

1a, b. Shift your balance onto your right foot, turning your body 90 degrees to your left, crossing both arms in front of your upper body.

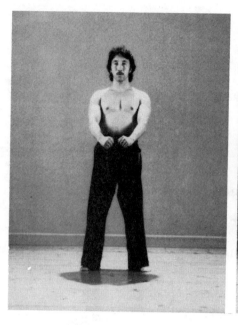

2c, d. Bringing your right foot back down, step into a right forward stance while simultaneously executing a right hand lunge punch.

2e. Immediately follow this with a left hand reverse punch.

1c. Stepping with your left foot, assume a right rear foot stance while simultaneously executing a double knifehand down block.

2a. Shift your balance onto your left foot, raise your right foot to chamber.

2b. Execute a front snap kick with your right foot.

3a. Shifting your balance onto your left leg, pivot on the ball of your left foot 180 degrees clockwise, crossing both arms in front of your upper chest.

3b. Stepping with your right foot, assume a left rear foot stance while simultaneously executing a double knifehand down block.

4a, b. Shift your balance onto your right foot, raise your left foot to chamber.

4c. Execute a front snap kick with your left foot.

5b. Stepping with your left foot, assume a left forward stance while simultaneously executing a knifehand high section block with your left hand and an inward high section knifehand chop with your right hand.

6a. Bringing your right hand in an arc in front of your body, execute a palm pushing block to the outside.

4d, e. Bringing your left foot back down, step into a left forward stance while simultaneously executing a left hand lunge punch.

4f. Immediately follow this with a right hand reverse punch.

5a. Shifting balance onto your right foot, pivot on the ball of your right foot 90 degrees to your left, raising your left hand 90 degrees to your side.

6b. Shifting your balance onto your left foot, step forward with your right leg.

6c. Assume a right forward stance while simultaneously executing a left hand reverse punch.

7a,b. Bringing your left hand in an arc in front of your body, execute a palm pushing block to the outside.

7c. Shifting your balance onto your right foot, step forward with your left leg.

7d. Assume a left forward stance while simultaneously executing a right hand reverse punch.

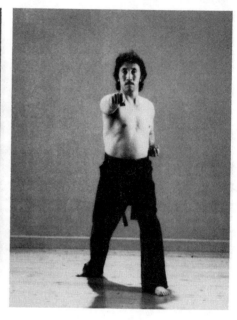

8d. Assume a right forward stance while simultaneously executing a left hand reverse punch. KI-HAP!

9a. Shifting balance onto your right leg, pivot 270 degrees counter-clockwise on the ball of your right foot while bringing both arms behind you.

9b. Stepping with your left foot, assume a right back stance while simultaneously executing a twin outer forearm block.

8a, b. Bringing your right hand in an arc in front of your body, execute a palm pushing block to the outside.

8c. Shifting your balance onto your left foot, step forward with your right leg.

10a, b. Maintaining the stance, rapidly pull your left arm inward to your shoulder while executing an uppercut with your right hand.

11a. Maintaining the stance, pull your left arm back into chamber position.

11b. Execute a side lunge punch with your left arm.

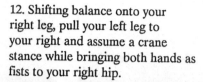

12. Shifting balance onto your right leg, pull your left leg to your right and assume a crane stance while bringing both hands as fists to your right hip.

13c, d. Immediately after the kick, bring your left leg down in front of you and assume a left forward stance while simultaneously executing an elbow strike with your right elbow into your left palm.

14a, b. Bring your left leg back to your right, and turning 180 degrees clockwise, step with your right foot into a left back stance, simultaneously executing a twin outer forearm block.

13a, b. After bringing your left leg into chamber position, execute a side kick.

15a, b. Maintaining the stance, rapidly pull your right arm inward to your shoulder while executing an uppercut with your left hand.

16a. Maintaining the stance, pull your right arm back into chamber position.

16b. Execute a side lunge punch with your right arm.

17a, b. Shifting balance onto your left leg, pull your right leg to your left and assume a crane stance while bringing both hands as fists to your left hip.

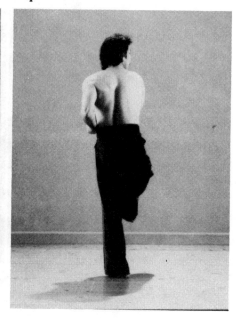

18c, d. Immediately after the kick, bring your right leg down in front of you and assume a right forward stance while simultaneously executing an elbow strike with your left elbow into your right palm.

19a. Shifting balance onto your left leg, bring your right foot to your left, bringing both arms behind you.

18a, b. After bringing your right leg into chamber position, execute a side kick.

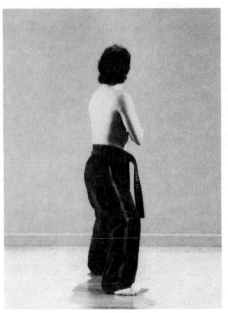

Front View

19b, c. Stepping forward with your left leg, assume a right back stance while simultaneously executing a knifehand guarding block.

20a, b. Shifting balance onto your left leg, step forward with your right foot and assume a right foward stance while simultaneously executing a spearfinger attack with your right hand.

21a. Pivoting on the ball of your right foot, turn 360 degrees counter-clockwise.

Front View

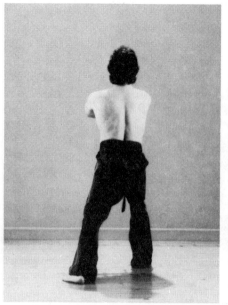

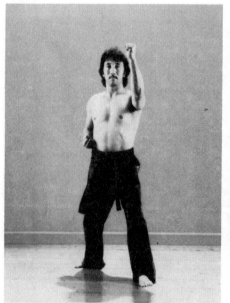

Front View

22a, b. Shifting balance onto your left leg, step forward and assume a right forward stance. Execute a right hand lunge punch and KI-HAP!

21b. Stepping forward with your left foot, assume a left forward stance while simultaneously executing a left hand back fist attack to the temple region.

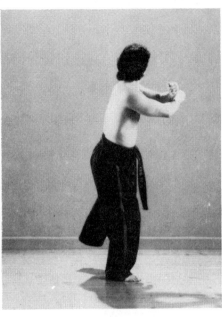
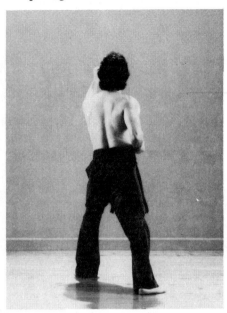

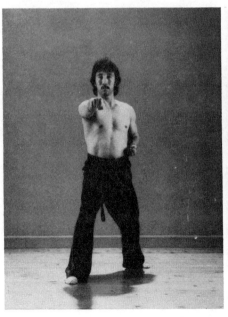

Front View

23a. Pivot on the ball of the right foot 270 degrees counter-clockwise while crossing both arms in front of your chest in an arcing motion, left arm closer to you.

23b, c. Stepping with the left foot, assume a left forward stance while continue moving your arms, executing a low section block with your left hand and an inner forearm block with your right hand.

24a. Maintaining your hand position, shift your balance onto your left foot and raise your right foot into chamber position.

24b. Execute a front snap kick with your right leg.

25a. Shifting balance onto your left leg, pivot 180 degrees clockwise on the ball of your left foot while crossing both arms in front of your chest in an arcing motion, right arm closer to you.

25b, c. Stepping with the right foot, assume a right forward stance while continue moving your arms, executing a low section block with your right hand and an inner forearm block with your left hand.

24c, d. Immediately after the kick, bring your right leg down in front of you and assume a right forward stance while simultaneously executing right hand lunge punch.

24e. Immediately follow with a left hand reverse punch.

26a. Maintaining your hand position, shift your balance onto your right foot and raise your left foot into chamber position.

26b. Execute a front snap kick with your left leg.

26c, d. Immediately after the kick, bring your left leg down in front of you and assume a left forward stance while simultaneously executing left hand lunge punch.

26e-g. Immediately follow with a right hand reverse punch.

Shift your balance onto your right foot and bring your left leg back to the ready position.

PYEONG-WON

PYEONG-WON HYUNG

Being civilized gradually, mankind migrated from the mountains to the plains in search of food. As a result the plains transfigured the environment and inspired in man a longing for peace and dominion over the land.

PYEONG-WON, which means "plains," is the most magnificent manifestation of good; an immense surface of earth spreading far in all directions. Because of this, the body positions of PYEONG-WON HYUNG are composed of movements to symbolize the simple power of the plains which stems from its divine connection to the earth.

The diagram of PYEONG-WON HYUNG is expressed by the symbol (-), like the shape of the plains. Even the movements of PYEONG-WON HYUNG represent joyous man dancing on the plains.

It is important to remember the basis of the movements in PYEONG-WON HYUNG, which is conservation of power and flexibility.

PYEONG-WON HYUNG

1a. Assume the ready position, feet together, arms straight and palms open.

1b, c. Crossing your arms in front of your face, palms open, slowly execute a twin knifehand down block.

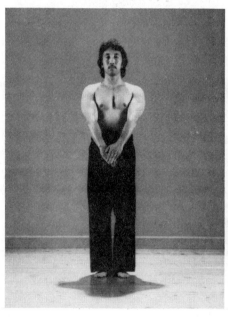

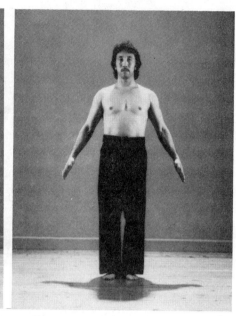

3b. Stepping forward with the right leg, assume a left back stance while executing a knifehand down block with the right hand.

4a. Shifting balance onto your right leg, turn your body 180 degrees to your left while crossing your left arm to the inside of your right arm.

4b. Adjusting your left foot, assume a right back stance while simultaneously executing a knifehand block with the left arm.

2a, b. Bringing both arms to your sides, slowly push outwards, bringing your hands to face level while exhaling strongly.

3a. Shifting balance onto your left leg, cross your right arm to the inside of your left arm.

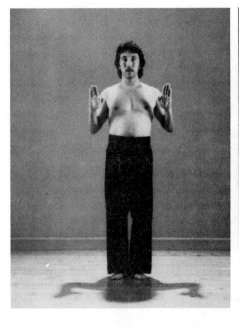

5a. Pick up your left foot slightly, sliding it one foot's length to the left while dropping your right hand to your side, fist closed.

5b. Changing your stance into a left forward stance, rapidly swing your right arm upward, executing an elbow strike to face level.

6a. Shifting balance onto your left leg, raise your right leg to chamber position.

6b. Execute a front snap kick with your right leg.

6c, d. Drop your kicking leg forward, immediately shifting balance onto it and pivoting on the ball of your right foot 180 degree counter-clockwise, raising your left leg to chamber position.

6g, h. Assume a right back stance while simultaneously executing a knifehand guarding block.

7a. Maintaining the stance, raise both arms in a giant arc over your head from front to back.

7b. Continuing this arcing motion, execute a twin knifehand low section block.

6e. Execute a back turning kick with your left leg

6f. Dropping the kicking leg down in front of you, raise both arms behind you.

8a, b. Raising both arms behind you, fists closed, execute a two arm block to the left side.

9a. Shifting balance onto your right foot, raise your left foot while reaching behind you with your left hand.

9b. Assuming a riding horse stance by stomping your left foot down, execute a backfist attack with your left arm while bringing your right fist to your left elbow, right fist closed and arm parallel to the ground.

10a. Shifting balance onto your left foot, raise your right foot while reaching behind you with your right hand.

10b. Assuming a riding horse stance by stomping your right foot down, execute a backfist attack with your right arm while bringing your left fist to your right elbow, left fist closed and arm parallel to the ground.

12b. Stomping your right foot down, execute a "W" shaped block.

13a. Shifting balance onto your left leg, bring your right foot to your left while crossing your right arm to the inside of your left to the side of your head.

13b. Assume a crane stance while simultaneously executing a high section block with your left arm and a low section block with your right arm.

11a. Shifting balance onto your right foot, lower your right arm on top of your left arm while stepping with your left foot towards your right.

11b. Step your left foot in front of your right and assume an "X" stance while executing a twin elbow attack with both arms.

12a. Shifting balance onto your left leg, raise your right foot while also raising both arms to your sides.

14. Bring your right leg into a solid chamber position.

15a. Execute a side kick with your right foot.

15b, c. Bring the kicking leg down in front of you, landing in a right forward stance while simultaneously executing an elbow strike with the left arm.

16a. Shifting balance onto your right leg, raise your left leg to chamber position.

16b. Execute a front snap kick with your left leg.

16f. Execute a back turning kick with your right leg.

16g. Dropping the kicking leg down in front of you, raise both arms behind you.

16h. Assume a left back stance while simultaneously executing a knifehand guarding block.

16c - e. Drop your kicking leg forward, immediately shifting balance onto it and pivoting on the ball of your left foot 180 degree clockwise, raising your right leg to chamber position.

17a. Maintaining the stance, raise both arms in a giant arc over your head from front to back.

17b. Continuing this arcing motion, execute a twin knifehand low section block.

18a, b. Raising both arms fists closed, execute a two arm block to the right side.

19a. Shifting balance onto your left foot, raise your right foot while reaching behind you with your right hand.

21a. Shifting balance onto your left foot, lower your left arm on top of your right arm while stepping with your right foot towards your left.

21b. Step your right foot in front of your left and assume an "X" stance while executing a twin elbow attack with both arms.

22a. Shifting balance onto your right leg, raise your left foot while also raising both arms to your sides.

19b. Assuming a riding horse stance by stomping your right foot down, execute a backfist attack with your right arm while bringing your left fist to your right elbow, left fist closed and arm parallel to the ground.

20a. Shifting balance onto your right foot, raise your left foot while reaching behind you with your left hand.

20b. Assuming a riding horse stance by stomping your left foot down, execute a backfist attack with your left arm while bringing your right fist to your left elbow, right fist closed and arm parallel to the ground.

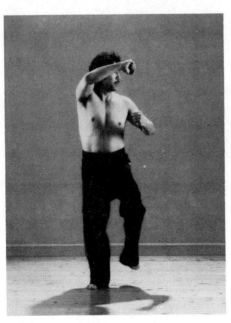

22b. Stomping your left foot down, execute a "W" shaped block.

23a, b. Shifting balance onto your right leg, bring your left foot to your right while crossing your left arm to the inside of your right by the side of your head.

23c. Assume a crane stance while simultaneously executing a high section block with your right arm and a low section block with your left arm.

24. Bring your left leg into a solid chamber position.

25a. Execute a side kick with your left foot.

25b, c. Bring the kicking leg down in front of you, landing in a left forward stance while simultaneously executing an elbow strike with the right arm.

Bring your left foot back to your right foot and assume the ready position.

SIP-JIN

SIP-JIN HYUNG

SIP JANG SANG orginally meant the worship of ten kinds of immortal things; sun, mountains, water, stone, the pine tree, the moon, the elixir of life, the tortoise, the crane and the deer. It is with this idea that SIP-JIN HYUNG was developed.

Much the same way that the infinite is composed of smaller steps, SIP-JIN HYUNG requires the ability to have a good command of endless changes of action in relation to body position.

This concept of endless change is expressed by the diagram (+), which represents immortality.

SIP-JIN HYUNG

Assume the ready position.

1a, b. Raise your arms from the ready position in a slow, powerful manner to a double rising block above your head.

3. Moving your left foot one foot's length to the left, assume a left forward stance while simultaneously executing a right spearhand attack.

4a, b. Immediately execute a left hand, mid-section lunge punch, followed by a right hand mid-section reverse punch.

2a. Shifting balance onto the right leg, cross your left arm to the inside of your right, to the side of your head.

2b. Stepping with the left leg, assume a right back stance while simultaneously executing an inner forearm block with the left arm while bringing the right hand, palm open to the left wrist.

3a. Opening the left hand, pivot it clockwise, executing a knife hand block.

5a, b. Shifting balance onto the left leg, raise the right leg and execute an outside to inside crescent kick.

5c, d. Bringing the kicking leg forward, assume a riding horse stance while executing a "W" shaped block.

6a, b. Shifting balance onto the right leg, cross your left leg behind your right while bringing your right fist to your hip.

7c. Stepping with your right foot, assume a riding horse stance while executing a twin elbow attack.

8a. Shifting balance onto the right leg, bring your left foot to your right while bringing your left hand, open palmed, to your right wrist.

8b. Stepping with your right foot, assume a left back stance while executing an inner forearm block with the right hand, keeping your left hand at your right wrist.

6c. Stepping with your right leg, assume a left back stance while executing a side punch with your right hand.

7a, b. Shifting balance onto the left leg, pivot 180 degrees counter-clockwise while crossing both arms in front of your chest.

8c. Opening the right hand, pivot it counter-clockwise, executing a knife hand block.

9. Moving your right foot one foot's length to the right, assume a right forward stance while simultaneously executing a left spearhand attack.

10a, b. Immediately execute a right hand, mid-section lunge punch, followed by a left hand mid-section reverse punch.

11a, b. Shifting balance onto the right leg, raise the left leg and execute an outside to inside crescent kick.

12a, b. Shifting balance onto the left leg, cross your right leg behind your left while bringing your left fist to your hip.

12c. Stepping with your left leg, assume a right back stance while executing a side punch with your left hand.

13a, b. Shifting balance onto the right leg, pivot 180 degrees clockwise while crossing both arms in front of your chest.

11c, d. Bringing the kicking leg forward, assume a riding horse stance while executing a "W" shaped block.

13c. Stepping with your left foot, assume a riding horse stance while executing a twin elbow attack.

14a. Shifting balance onto the left leg, pivot 90 degrees clockwise while raising your left hand, open palmed, to your right wrist.

14b. Assume a left back stance while executing an inner forearm block with the right hand, keeping your left hand at your right wrist.

15a. Moving the right foot one foot's length to the right, assume a right forward stance while pushing your right hand forward into a spearhand attack.

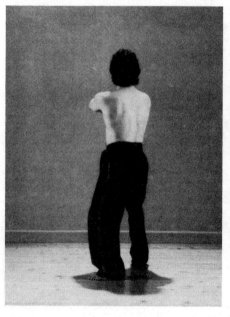

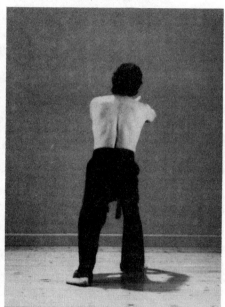

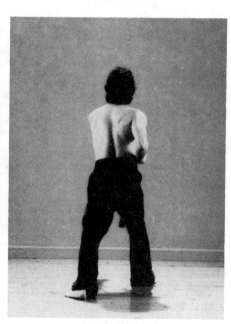

Front View

16a. Immediately execute a right hand lunge punch.

16b. Maintaining the stance, execute a left hand reverse punch.

15b. Maintaining the stance, execute a left hand spearhand attack.

Front View

Front View

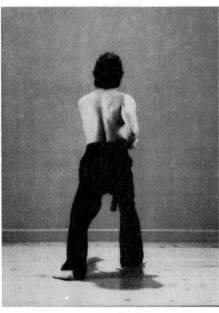

Front View

17a. Shifting balance onto the right leg, step forward with the left foot, raise both hands behind you.

17b. Stepping with the left foot, assume a right back stance while simultaneously executing a twin knifehand down block.

Front View

18a. Shifting balance onto the left leg, bring both hands, open palmed to your sides.

18b. Step forward with the right foot, assuming a right forward stance while simultaneously executing a pushing block with both hands.

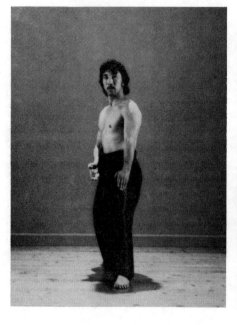

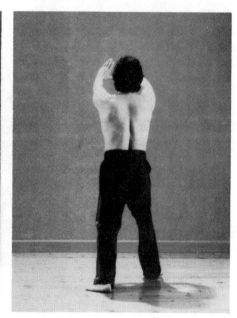

20a. Bringing your right foot on foot's length to your left, cross both arms in front of your face.

20b. Assuming a ready stance, execute a twin low section block.

21a. Shifting balance onto the right leg, pivot 90 degrees on the ball of your right foot while extending your left arm out to your side.

123

Front View

19a. Shifting balance onto the left leg, raise the right leg and turn 90 degrees to the left, crossing both arms.

19b. Assuming a riding horse stance, execute twin knifehand wedging blocks

21b, c. Stepping with your left foot, assume a left forward stance while simultaneously executing a circular punch with your left arm.

22a. Maintaining the stance, bring both hands, palms open, to your right side.

22b. Pushing slowly forward, execute a pushing block.

23a. Shifting balance onto the left leg, raise the right leg to chamber position.

23b. Execute a front snap kick with the right leg.

24b. Execute a front snap kick with the left leg.

24c. Drop the kicking leg down in front of you, bringing both hands to your right side.

24d. Stepping into a left forward stance, execute an uneven punch.

23c. Drop the kicking leg down in front of you, bringing both hands to your left side.

23d. Stepping into a right forward stance, execute an uneven punch.

24a. Shifting balance onto the right leg, raise the left leg to chamber position.

25a. Shifting balance onto the left leg, raise the right leg to chamber position.

25b. Execute a front snap kick with the right leg.

25c. Drop the kicking leg forward, immediately shifting balance onto it while bringing both hands behind you.

25d. Hopping forward with the left foot, assume a right "X" stance while executing a back fist attack with your right hand and a guarding block with your left hand.

26a. Keeping the balance on your right foot, pivot 180 degrees on the ball of the right foot while lifting the left foot and raising both arms to your sides.

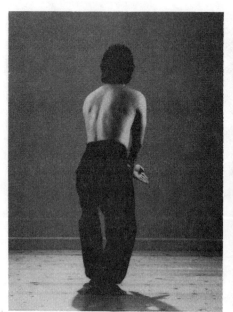

27b. Assume a right rear foot stance while executing a knifehand "X" block.

Front View

27a. Shifting balance onto the left leg, step forward with the right while bringing both arms behind you.

26b. Stepping with your left foot into a left forward stance, execute a pushing block with both hands.

Front View

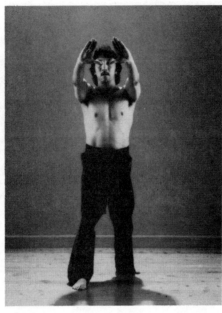

27a. Pull the left foot back to the right, raising both arms to your sides, palms open.

27b. Assume left back stance while simultaneously executing an inner ridgehand block with the right hand and a guarding block with the left hand.

Front View

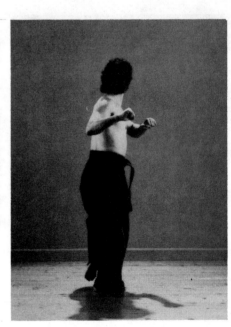

28a. Shifting balance onto the right leg, step forward with the left while bringing both arms behind you.

128

28b. Assume a right back stance while simultaneously executing an uneven punch.

Front View

29a. Shifting balance onto the left leg, step forward with the right while bringing both arms behind you.

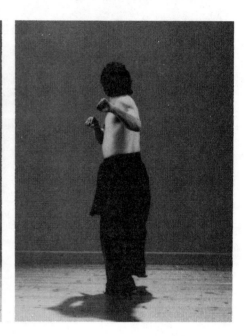

29b. Assume a left back stance while simultaneously executing an uneven punch.

Front View

Shifting balance onto your right leg, pivot 90 degrees to your left side and return to the ready position.

JI-TAE

JI-TAE HYUNG

    On the earth every creature is born, grows up and dies off as does the wind which causes the changing of the seasons.

    JI-TAE, the symbol for the earth, not only represents a supportive and nurturing enviornment given to us by heaven, but also represents the universal principle of doing without doing. Much the same way that the wind when moved can topple trees, the earth actively sustains us by its very presence. It is this idea of action without effort which gives birth to the JI-TAE HYUNG body positions.

    The main concept behind some of the movements in JI-TAE HYUNG is to bring a sense of grand thought and concentration to the motions of the body. This is expressed by a slowing of several of the movements so that the power of each of these movements is felt by degrees.

JI-TAE HYUNG

Assume the ready position.

1a. Shifting balance onto your right leg, turn 90 degrees to your left while crossing your left arm to the outside of your right arm.

1b. Stepping forward with your left foot, assume a right back stance while simultaneously executing an inner forearm block with your left arm.

3a. Shifting balance onto your left leg, turn 180 degrees to your right while crossing your right arm to the outside of your left.

3b. Stepping forward with your right foot, assume a left back stance while simultaneously executing an inner forearm block with your right arm.

4a. Shifting balance onto your right leg, move forward while crossing your left arm to the inside of your right.

2a. Shifting balance onto your left leg, move forward while crossing your right arm to the inside of your left.

2b. Stepping forward with the right leg, assume a right forward stance while executing a slow, high section block with the right arm.

2c. Immediately execute a left hand reverse punch.

4b. Stepping forward with the left leg, assume a left forward stance while executing a slow, high section block with the left arm.

4c. Immediately execute a right hand reverse punch.

5a. Shifting balance onto your right leg, turn 90 degrees to your left while crossing your left arm to the inside of your right.

5b. Stepping forward with the left foot, assume a left forward stance while executing a low section block with the left arm.

6a. Shifting balance onto your right foot, begin to pull your left foot towards the right while crossing both arms, left arm to the inside.

6b. Assume a right back stance while simultaneously executing a knifehand, high section block with your left hand.

7d. Assume a left back stance while executing a twin knifehand down block.

8a. Maintaining the stance, cross your right arm to the outside of your left arm.

8b. Execute an outer forearm block with your right arm.

7a. Shifting balance onto your left leg, raise your right leg to chamber position.

7b. Execute a front snap kick with your right leg.

7c. Immediately after the kick, drop your kicking leg down in front of you, raising both arms behind.

9a. Shifting balance onto your right leg, raise your left leg to chamber position.

9b. Execute a front snap kick with your left leg.

9c. Immediately after the kick, drop your kicking leg down in front of you, raising both arms behind.

9d. Assume a right back stance while executing a twin knifehand down block.

10a. Shifting balance onto your right leg, move your left foot one foot's length to the left while crossing your left arm to the inside of your right.

10b. Assuming a left forward stance, execute a slow, high section block with the left arm.

12b. Execute an inner forearm block with your left arm.

12c. Maintaining the stance, raise your right arm 90 degrees to your side.

12d. Execute an inner forearm block with your right arm.

137

11a, b. Shifting balance onto your left leg, step forward into a right forward stance while simultaneously executing both a high section block with the right arm and a reverse punch with the left arm.

12a. Maintaining the stance, raise your left arm 90 degrees to your side.

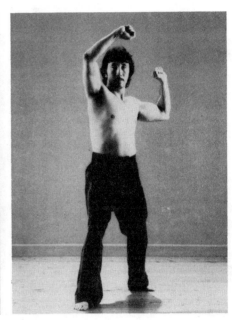

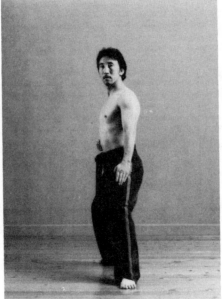

13a. Shifting balance onto your left leg, step backwards with your right foot while crossing your left arm to the inside of your right.

13b. Assuming a right back stance, execute a knifehand down block with your left arm.

14a. Shifting balance onto your left leg, raise your right leg to chamber position.

14b. Execute a front snap kick with your right leg.

14c - e. Immediately after the kick, bring your kicking leg back behind you so that you assume a left forward stance. Simultaneously execute a right hand reverse punch,

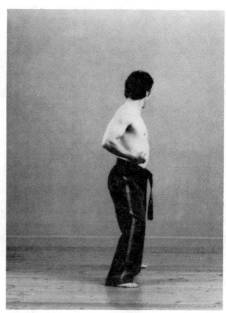

bringing both hands over your head, elbows bent, fists tight and close together, facing outward.

16a. Maintaining the stance, cross your left arm to the inside of your right.

16b. Execute a low section block with the left arm.

followed by a left hand lunge punch. All of these moves should happen quickly, one right after another.

15a - c. Shifting balance onto your right leg, move your left foot backwards and assume a riding horse stance while simultaneously

Front View

17a. Maintaining the stance, cross the right arm to the inside of the left.

17b. Execute an outer knifehand block with the right arm.

18. Maintaining the stance, bring the left fist in a circular manner into the right open hand.

19a. Shifting balance onto your left leg, raise your right leg while crossing your right arm to the inside of your left arm.

19b. Assume a crane stance while executing a low section block with the right hand.

21c. Shifting balance onto your right foot, raise your left leg and assume a crane stance while executing a low section block with your left hand.

Front View

22. Maintaining the stance, bring both hands to your right hip.

141

20. Maintaining the stance, bring both hands to your left hip.

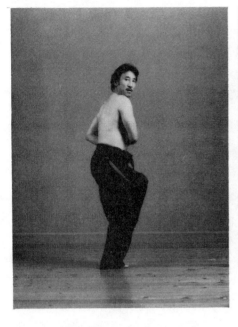

21a. Execute a side kick with your right leg.

21b. Drop the kicking leg directly next to your balance leg while crossing your left arm to the inside of your right arm and turning your head 180 degrees to your left

23a. Execute a side kick with your left leg.

23b, c. Dropping the kicking leg forward assume a left forward

stance while simultaneously executing a right hand reverse punch.

Front View

24a. Shifting balance onto your left leg, bring your right hand back to your hip.

24b. Stepping forward, assume a right forward stance and execute a right hand lunge punch. KI-HAP!

26a. Shifting balance onto your left foot, step forward with your right foot while raising both arms behind you.

26b. Stepping forward, assume a left back stance while executing a knifehand guarding block.

27a. Shifting balance onto your left leg, pivot 180 degrees clockwise on the ball of your left foot while raising both arms behind you.

Front View

25a. Shifting balance onto your right leg, pivot 270 degrees counter-clockwise on the ball of your right foot while raising both arms behind you.

25b. Assuming a right back stance, execute a twin, knifehand down block.

27b. Assuming a left back stance, execute a twin, knifehand down block.

28a. Shifting balance onto your right foot, step forward with your left foot while raising both arms behind you.

28b. Stepping forward, assume a right back stance while executing a knifehand guarding block.

Shifting balance onto your right foot, pivot 180 degrees counter-clockwise and return to the ready position.

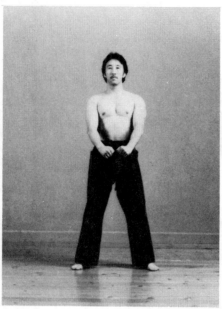

147

CHEON-KWON

CHEON-KWON HYUNG

Heaven is defined as the basis of nature as well as the perfect central point around which all things in the universe revolve. This is CHEON-KWON. As an infinite, profound and imaginable world ruled by the creator of the universe, CHEON-KWON is not only a visible, semi-circular space high overhead, but is itself regarded as a god to be worshiped by our softer human nature.

Accordingly, CHEON-KWON HYUNG is composed of movements extracted from a sense of an infinite and profound heaven. This pattern can also be represented by the diagram (⊥), as if one were staring up at heaven from the earth.

CHEON-KWON HYUNG

Assume a closed ready position, feet together, arms straight and palms open.

1. Slowly raise both hands to your chest while inhaling deeply.

2. Extending your hands outward in a pushing motion, exhale.

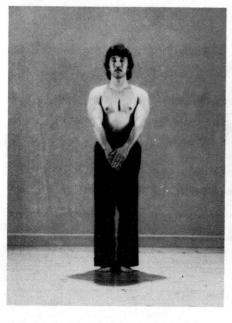

3d. Bring both hands in an arcing manner to your sides, closing your fists, middle knuckles extended and moving your left foot slightly behind your right.

3e. Assume a left back stance while simultaneously executing a twin upward knuckle punch.

4a. Shifting balance onto your right leg, pick up your left foot and extend it backwards at a 45 degree angle, while crossing your left arm to the inside of your right arm.

3a - c. Bring both hands in an arcing manner downward towards the floor and then upwards, crossing the arms as you continue the arcing motion until you are in an overhead "bull" block.

4b. Assuming a right forward stance, execute a knifehand block with your left hand.

5a. Shifting balance onto your right foot, step forward while turning your left hand as if you were grabbing an opponent's wrist.

5b. Assuming a left forward stance, execute a reverse punch with your right hand.

6a. Shifting balance onto your left leg, pick up your right foot and slide it sideways to a 45 degree angle, while crossing your right arm to the inside of your left arm.

6b. Assuming a left forward stance, execute a knifehand block with your right hand.

7a. Shifting balance onto your left foot, step forward while turning your right hand as if you were grabbing an opponent's wrist.

9a. Shifting balance onto your right foot, raise your left foot to chamber position.

9b. Execute a side kick with the left leg.

9c. Drop the kicking leg down in front of you while crossing your left arm to the inside of your right arm.

7b. Assuming a right forward stance, execute a reverse punch with your left hand.

8a. Shifting balance onto your right leg, pick up your left foot and slide it sideways to a 45 degree angle, while crossing your left arm to the inside of your right arm.

8b. Assuming a right forward stance, execute a knifehand block with your left hand.

9d. Assume a left forward stance while executing a low section block with your left arm.

10a. Shifting balance onto your left foot, step forward with your right leg.

10b. Assuming a right forward stance, execute a lunge punch with your right hand.

11a. Shifting balance onto your right leg, pivot 270 degrees counter-clockwise on the ball of your right foot, raising both fists beind you.

11b. Stepping with your left foot, assume a right back stance while simultaneously executing an inner forearm block with your left hand and a guarding block with your right.

13b. Shifting balance onto your left foot step forward while raising the left hand into a knifehand high section block.

12a - d. Maintaining the stance, first pull the left hand sharply towards you, and then making a big counter-clockwise arc with your arm, pull it back to your left side and execute a side punch.

13a. Again, pull the hand sharply towards you.

13c. Stepping with the right foot, assume a left back stance, simultaneously executing a side punch with the right hand.

14a. Shifting balance onto your left leg, pivot 180 degrees clockwise on the ball of your left foot, raising both fists beind you.

14b. Stepping with your right foot, assume a left back stance while simultaneously executing an inner forearm block with your right hand and a guarding block with your left.

Front View

15a - d. Maintaining the stance, first pull the right hand sharply towards you, and then making a big clockwise arc with your arm, pull it back to your right side and execute a side punch.

16b. Shifting balance onto your right foot step forward while raising the right hand into a knifehand high section block.

16c. Stepping with the left foot, assume a right back stance, simultaneously executing a side punch with the left hand.

17a. Shifting balance onto your right foot, pivot 90 degrees to your left side.

16a. Again, pull the hand sharply towards you.

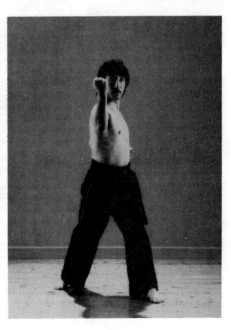

Front View

17b. Stepping with your left foot, assume a left forward stance while crossing your right arm to the inside of your left arm.

17c. Execute an inner forearm block with the right arm, twisting your body 90 degrees away from the block to the left.

18. Maintaining the stance, execute a lunge punch with the left hand.

19a. Shifting balance onto your left leg, raise the right leg to chamber position.

Front View

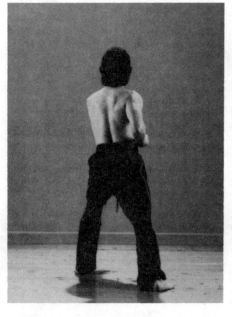

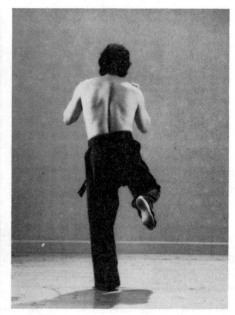

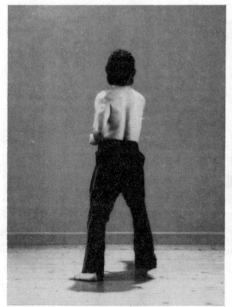

simultaneoulsy executing a lunge punch with the right hand.

Front View

20a. Shifting balance onto your left leg, pull your right foot back towards the left while raising both arms behind you.

19b. Execute a front snap kick with the right leg.

19c, d. Immediately after the kick, drop the kicking leg forward while

Front View

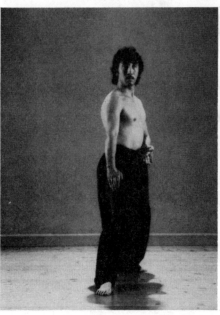
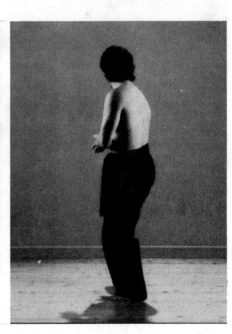

20b. Assume a left back stance while executing a twin, knifehand down block.

Front View

21a - c. After first moving your right foot forward one foot's length, slide your left foot forward an equal distance and simultaneously execute an inner forearm block with your right arm and a guarding block with your left arm as you skip slightly forward.

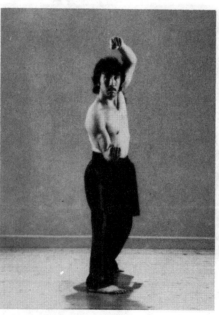

you and execute a "U" shaped punch with both hands.

Front View

23a - c. Springing off of the balls of both feet, execute a jumping 360 degree outside to inside crescent kick with the right foot.

21d. Skipping forward again, maintain the stance and immediately follow this with a twin low section block.

Front View

22a, b. Shifting your right foot into a horse riding stance position, bring both arms behind

23d. Landing in a riding horse stance, execute another "U" shaped punch.

Front View

24a. Turning your head 180 degrees to the left, assume a right back stance while crossing your right arm to the inside of your left arm.

24b. Execute a knifehand down block with the left hand and a high section ridgehand block with the right.

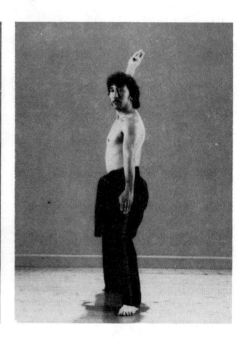

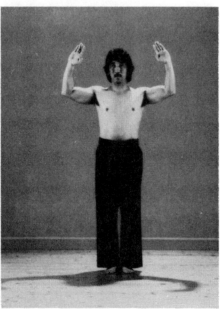

26b. Bring both hands in an arcing manner downward towards the floor and then upwards, until you are in an overhead "bull" block.

26c. Pivoting 90 degrees to your right side, bring both hands to your sides.

25a. Turning your upper body 180 degrees to your right, cross your right arm to the inside of your left arm.

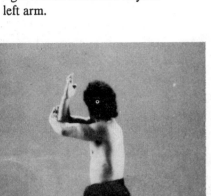

25b. Execute a knifehand down block with the right hand and a high section ridgehand block with the left while shifting your feet into a left back stance position.

26a. Shifting balance onto your right foot, turn 90 degrees to the left while you slowly raise both hands to your chest in a circular motion, inhaling deeply.

26d. Stepping forward with the right foot, assume a left back stance while simultaneously executing a pole block with both hands.

27a. Bringing the right foot back to the left, push both hands slowly upwards, assuming another overhead "bull" block.

27b. Pivoting 90 degrees to your left side, bring both hands to your sides.

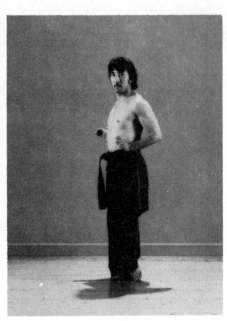

27c. Stepping forward with the left foot, assume a right back stance while simultaneously executing a pole block with both hands.

27d. Bring the left foot back to the right foot and assume a closed,

ready stance, feet together, arms straight and palms open.

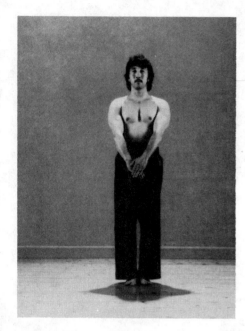

HAN-SOO

HAN-SOO HYUNG

Water is the most basic element in the universe, yet it has neither smell, taste nor color. Although water in small amounts appears weak, the power of a large quantity, once gathered, is inconceivably strong.

The main concept behind HAN-SOO HYUNG arises from the fact that water gathered drop by drop can form a mighty river. This is a truth that all people must appreciate.

The characteristics of water is that it cannot be cut, it is fluid. Water is also very adaptable; its shape is subject to change according to the shape of its receptacle. Water's strength on one hand and its adaptability on the other hand demonstrates a unified spirit which keeps in touch with the spirit of Tae Kwon Do, as well as all human life.

The diagram of HAN-SOO HYUNG is represented by 「水」 which symbolizes the concept of fluidity as well as incredible power. While practicing HAN-SOO HYUNG, one should try to cultivate the ability to have a good command of both offensive and defensive body positions.

HAN-SOO HYUNG

Assume a closed ready position, feet together, arms straight and palms open.

1a. Shifting balance onto your right foot, cross arms against your chest, left arm on top and both hands open.

1b. Stepping with your left foot, assume a left forward stance while simultaneously executing a ridgehand wedging block.

3b. Stepping backward with the right foot, assume a right forward stance, however keep your upper body facing in the previous direction. Simultaneously, execute a down block with the left hand and a back fist attack with the right.

4a. Shifting balance onto your right foot, move your left foot one foot's length to the left, simultaneously bringing your right hand to your right hip.

4b. Assuming a left forward stance, execute a right hand reverse punch.

2a. Shifting balance onto your left foot, raise both hands to your sides.

2b. Stepping with your right foot, assume a right forward stance, simultaneously executing a twin, inward hammerfist strike.

3a. Shifting balance onto your left foot, start to step backwards with your right foot while crossing your left arm to the top of your right.

5a. Shifting balance onto your right foot, start to step backwards with your left foot while crossing your right arm to the top of your left.

5b. Stepping backward with the left foot, assume a left forward stance, however keep your upper body facing in the previous direction. Simultaneously, execute a down block with the right hand and a back fist attack with the left..

6a. Shifting balance onto your left foot, move your right foot one foot's length to the right, simultaneously bringing your left hand to your left hip.

6b. Assuming a right forward stance, execute a left hand reverse punch.

7a. Shifting balance onto your left foot, start to step backwards with your right foot while crossing your left arm to the top of your right.

7b. Stepping backward with the right foot, assume a right forward stance, however keep your upper body facing in the previous direction. Simultaneously, execute a down block with the left hand and a back fist attack with the right.

9b. Stepping with the right foot, assume a right forward stance while simultaneously executing a ridgehand wedging block.

10a. Pivoting 45 degrees counter-clockwise on the ball of the right foot, shift your weight onto your right foot and step forward with your left, bringing both hands to either side of your waist, palms open.

10b. Stepping with the left foot, assume a left forward stance, simultaneously executing an arc hand attack with the left hand.

8a. Shifting balance onto your right foot, move your left foot one foot's length to the left, simultaneously bringing your right hand to your right hip.

8b. Assuming a left forward stance, execute a right hand reverse punch.

9a. Shifting balance onto your left foot, step forward with the right while crossing your left arm to the top of your right arm.

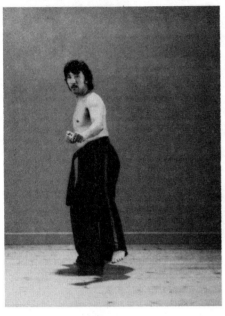

11a. Keeping at this angle, shift balance onto your left foot and begin to move your right foot forward while bringing both hands to either side of your waist, fists tight and palms facing downward.

11b, c. Hopping forward with the right foot, immediately bring the left foot along side of it into a bent knee closing stance. Simultaneoulsy execute a twin upset punch with both hands.

12a. Shifting balance onto your right foot, step your left foot backwards while raising both hands to either side, right hand as a fist and left hand open.

12b. Still keeping the 45 degree angle, step with the left foot and assume a riding horse stance, simultaneously executing an inner wrist low section block by bringing your right wrist into your open left hand.

13a. Shifting balance onto your left foot, step backwards with your right while crossing your left arm to the top of your right arm, palms open.

15a. Execute a left leg side kick.

15b. Immediately after the kick, drop the kicking leg forward while bringing your right hand behind you, palm open.

15c. Assuming a left forward stance, execute a knifehand high section block with your left hand and an inward knifehand strike with your right.

13b. Stepping with your right foot, assume a right back stance while executing a knifehand down block with your left hand and a knifehand high section block with your right.

14a, b. Shifting balance onto your right foot, pivot 45 degrees counter-clockwise, raising your left leg to a crane stance while bringing both hands as fists to your right hip.

16a. Maintaining hand position, shift your weight onto your left foot, raising your right foot to chamber position.

16b. Execute a front snap kick with your right foot.

16c - e. Immediately following the kick, drop your kicking leg forward, hopping forward onto your right foot and then bringing your left foot towards and behind your right foot, assuming an "X" stance. Simultaneously execute a back fist attack to face level with your right hand.

17a. Shifting balance onto your right foot, pivot 90 degrees counter-clockwise on the ball of your right foot while crossing your left arm to the top of your right arm, palm open.

18c. Immediately after the kick, drop the kicking leg forward.

18d. Assuming a riding horse stance, execute an elbow attack with your right elbow into your open left hand.

19a. Shifting balance onto your right foot, bring your left foot to your right, simultaneously bringing both hands to either side of your waist, palms open.

17b. Assuming a riding horse stance, execute a knifehand strike with your left hand.

18a. Shifting balance onto your left foot, begin to swing your right foot while turning your left hand to face into the direction of your right foot.

18b. Execute an outside to inside crescent kick to your left palm.

19b. Stepping with the right foot, assume a right forward stance, simultaneously executing an arc hand attack with the right hand with the left hand supporting the right arm below the elbow.

20a. Keeping at this angle, shift balance onto your right foot and begin to move your left foot forward while bringing both hands to either side of your waist, fists tight and palms facing downward.

20b, c. Hopping in with the left foot, immediately bring the right foot along side of it into a bent knee closing stance.

Simultaneoulsy execute a twin upset punch with both hands.

21a. Shifting balance onto your left foot, step your right foot backwards while raising both hands to either side, left hand as a fist and right hand open.

23a, b. Shifting balance onto your left foot, pivot 45 degrees clockwise, raising your right leg to a crane stance while bringing both hands as fists to your left hip.

21b. Still keeping the 45 degree angle, step with the right foot and assume a riding horse stance, simultaneously executing an inner wrist low section block by bringing your left wrist into your open right hand.

22a. Shifting balance onto your right foot, step backwards with your left while crossing your right arm to the top of your left arm, palms open.

22b. Stepping with your left foot, assume a left back stance while executing a knifehand down block with your right hand and a knifehand high section block with your left.

24a, b. Execute a right leg side kick.

24c. Immediately after the kick, drop the kicking leg forward while bringing your left hand behind you, palm open.

24d. Assuming a right forward stance, execute a knifehand high section block with your right hand and an inward knifehand strike with your left.

25a. Maintaining hand position, shift your weight onto your right foot, raising your left foot to chamber position.

25b. Execute a front snap kick with your left foot.

25c - f. Immediately following the kick, drop your kicking leg forward, hopping forward onto your left foot and then bringing your

26a. Shifting balance onto your left foot, pivot 90 degrees clockwise on the ball of your left foot while crossing your right arm to the top of your left arm, palm open.

26b. Assuming a riding horse stance, execute a knifehand strike with your right hand.

27a. Shifting balance onto your right foot, begin to swing your left foot while turning your right hand to face into the direction of your left foot.

right foot towards and behind your left foot, assuming an "X" stance. Simultaneously execute a back fist attack to face level with your left hand.

27b. Execute an outside to inside crescent kick to your right palm.

27c. Immediately after the kick, drop the kicking leg forward.

27d. Assuming a riding horse stance, execute an elbow attack with your left elbow into your open right hand.

Pivoting 45 degrees clockwise on the ball of your left foot, return to the closed ready stance position.

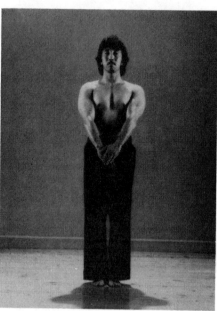

IL-YEO

IL-YEO HYUNG

    IL-YEO HYUNG derives its name from the central idea of Won Hyo who was the most reknowned Buddhist monk of the Silla Dynasty.

    The main concept of IL-YEO is that the mind (the spiritual) and the body (the physical) are not separable. In other words, there exists nothing but the one, much the same that a multitude of shapes - triangles, squares, circles, etc. - are no more than the continuation of a single point. With this in mind, the spiritual and the physical are turned into one thing by applying profound thought to IL-YEO HYUNG.

    The important characteristic of the body positions in IL-YEO HYUNG is the placing of emphasis on the coincidence of mind and body by using balance and symmetry so that you can reach the stage of self-effacement that is connected directly with the principle of IL-YEO.

IL-YEO HYUNG

Assume a closed ready stance with both arms raised in front, right fist inside left palm.

1a. Shifting balance onto your right foot, step forward with the left and raise both hands behind you.

1b. Assuming a right back stance, execute a knifehand guarding block.

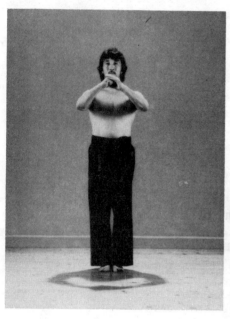

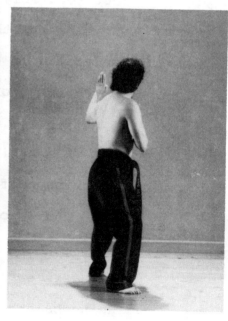

3b. Assuming a right back stance, execute a low section block with your left hand and a high section block with your right.

4a. Shifting balance onto your right foot, pivot 90 degrees counter-clockwise while raising both hands behind you.

4b. Stepping with your left foot, assume a right back stance while simultaneously executing a knifehand guarding block.

2a. Shifting balance onto your left foot, move your right foot forward while bringing your right fist to your right hip.

2b. Stepping with your right foot, assume a right forward stanace, simultaneously executing a lunge punch with your right hand.

3a. Pivoting 90 degrees counter-clockwise on the ball of the right foot, move the left foot forward while crossing your left arm to the top of your right arm.

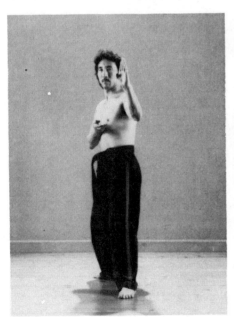

Front View

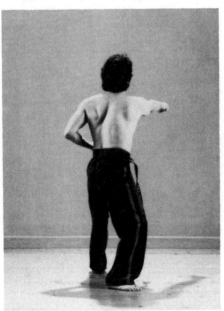

5. Maintaining the stance, execute a reverse punch with the right hand.

6a. Shifting balance onto your left foot, hop forward with your right foot.

6b. Maintaining the hopping motion, bring both hands to either side of your waist as you land forward on your right foot.

6c. Bringing your left instep to the back of your right leg, assume a crane stance while simultaneously executing a spearfinger attack to the solar plexus with your left hand.

Front View

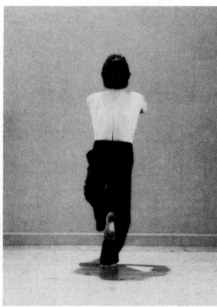

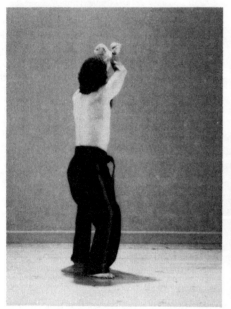

8b. Assume a right back stance while simultaneously executing an "X" rising block, right hand closer to your body.

9a. Pivot both hands around the point where the wrists are touching, opening the hands.

9b. Shifting balance onto your left foot, bring your right fist to your right side as you move your right foot forward.

185

7a. Pivoting on the ball of your right foot, raise your left leg to chamber position.

7b. Execute a side kick with the left leg.

8a. Immediately after executing the kick, drop the kicking leg down in front of you, bringing both hands as fists to either side of your waist.

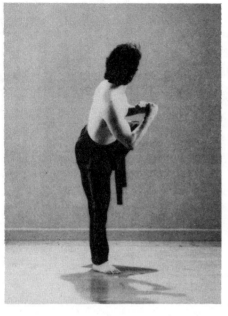

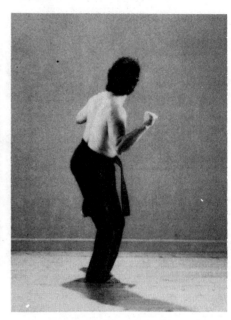

Front View

9c. Assume a right forward stance while simultaneously executing a lunge punch with the right hand.

10a. Shifting balance onto your right foot, pivot 90 degrees counter-clockwise while crossing your left arm to the top of your right arm.

10b. Stepping with the left foot, assume a right back stance while simultaneously executing a low section block with the left hand and a high section block with the right.

11a. Shifting balance onto your right foot, pivot 90 degrees counter-clockwise while raising both arms behind you.

11b. Stepping with the left foot, assume a right back stance while simultaneously executing a knifehand guarding block.

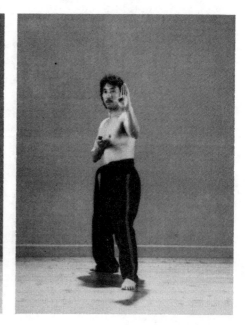

14a. Raise your left leg to chamber position, looking to your immediate left.

14b. Execute a side kick with the left leg.

15a. Immediately after executing the kick, drop the kicking leg down in front of you, bringing both hands as fists to either side.

187

12. Maintaining the stance, execute a reverse punch with the right hand.

13a. Shifting balance onto your left foot, hop forward with your right foot, bringing both hands to either side of your waist.

13c. As you land on the right foot, bring your left instep to the back of your right leg, assuming a crane stance while simultaneously executing a spearfinger attack to the solar plexus with your right hand.

15b. Assume a right back stance while simultaneously executing an "X" rising block, right hand closer to your body.

16a. Pivot both hands around the point where the wrists are touching, opening the hands.

16b. Shifting balance onto your left foot, bring your right fist to your right side as you move your right foot forward.

16c. Assume a right forward stance while simultaneously executing a lunge punch with the right hand.

17a. Shifting balance onto your right foot, pivot 90 degrees counter-clockwise while crossing your left arm to the top of your right arm.

17b. Stepping with the left foot, assume a right back stance while simultaneously executing a low section block with the left hand and a high section block with the right.

19b. Execute a front snap kick with the left leg.

19c,d. After first dropping the kicking leg down in front of you, spring off of the left foot and pivot 180 degrees counter-clockwise, raising your right leg into chamber position.

18a. Shifting balance onto your right foot, pivot 180 degrees counter-clockwise, crossing both hands in front of your body.

18b. Assume a closing stance while simultaneously bringing both hands as fists to either side of your waist, palms facing upwards.

19a. Shifting balance onto your right foot, raise your left foot into chamber position.

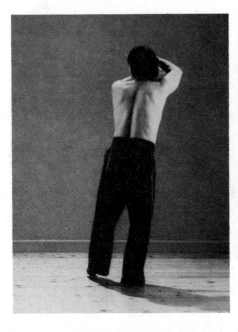
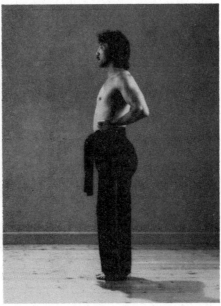

19e, f. Execute a jumping side kick with the right leg.

19g. Immediately after the kick, drop the kicking leg forward and raise both hands to either side of your body.

19h. Assume a left back stance while simultaneously executing an "X" rising block, right hand closer to your body.

20a. Pivot both hands around the point where the wrists are touching, opening the hands.

20b. Shifting balance onto your right foot, bring your left fist to your left side as you move your left foot forward.

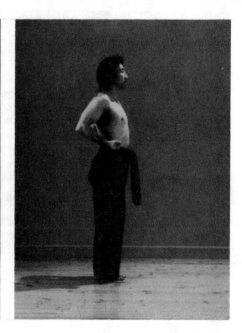

22a. Shifting balance onto your left foot, bring your right foot to your left while raising both arms above you.

22b, c. Assume a closing stance while simultaneously bringing both hands as fists to either side, palms facing upwards.

23a. Shifting balance onto your left foot, raise your right leg into chamber position.

20c. Assume a left forward stance while simultaneously executing a lunge punch with the left hand.

21a. Shifting balance onto your left foot, pivot 270 degrees clockwise while crossing your right arm to the top of your left arm.

21b. Stepping with the right foot, assume a left back stance while simultaneously executing a low section block with the right hand and a high section block with the left.

23b. Execute a front snap kick with the right leg.

23c - g. After first dropping the kicking leg down in front of you, execute a rear leg roundhouse kick with the left leg.

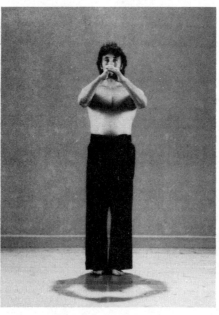

Shifting balance onto your right foot, bring your left foot to your right and assume a closed, ready stance, right fist inside of left hand.

23h. Immediately after the kick, drop the kicking leg forward and raise both hands to either side of your body.

23i. Assume a right back stance while simultaneously executing an "X" rising block, right hand closer to your body.

THE ORIENTAL METHOD OF FIRST AID USING TRADITIONAL ACUPUNCTURE POINTS

In addition to the martial arts, the orient's other great export to the west has been acupuncture. Studied and used in this country for several decades now, acupuncture has gotten increased respect as a legitimate healing art.

It is not surprising to discover that acupuncture points have been used widely by martial artists in the the orient for many years, both for the purpose of first aid and for general relaxation and health. While a number of different methods and techniques will be described over the next few pages, they are in no way meant to take the place of competent medical attention in the case of an emergency or accident.

There are literally dozens of acupuncture points located over the body, each one serving a different and distinct function. The points are actually channels; located on the skin and tying directly into the nervous system. Acupuncture is usually seen being performed using small needles (which are used to stimulate the points), but wonderful results can be obtained by simply applying direct, firm pressure to the point with the tip of the thumb or index finger. This pressure can either be applied by yourself (if possible in the situation) or by others.

There are two suggested methods of applying this pressure. The first one - apply pressure directly to the point for three to five seconds, then remove pressure for three to five seconds. This pressure on/pressure off method should be continued until you achieve the desired result. The second method is to apply and maintain direct pressure until you achieve the desired result.

Following are some revival points that can be used in the event a person becomes unconscious (knocked-out) or light-headed. They can be used individually, or in any combination.

1. GV-26:
Governing channel point #26 located in the philtrum, ⅓ the distance from bottom of nose to top of the upper lip.

2. LI-4:
Large Intestine channel point #4 located in the web between thumb and index finger. With thumb and index finger opened as wide as possible, locate the point slightly on the side of index finger between 1st & 2nd metacarpal bones.

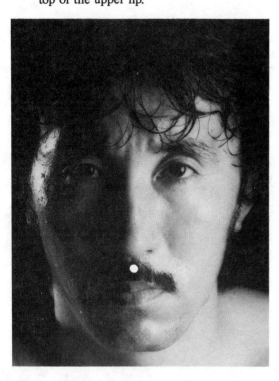

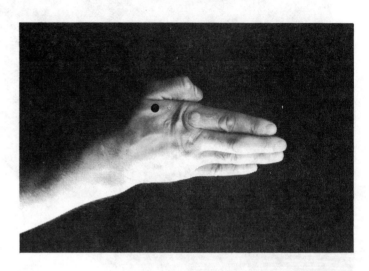

4. ST-36:
Stomach channel point #36 located on lower leg, approximately 4 finger width below the hollow next to patellar tendon below the knee.

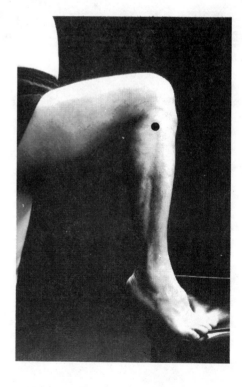

3. K-1:
Kidney channel point #1 located on the bottom of the foot, ⅓ the distance from base of 2nd toe to the edge of heel.

5. P-9:
Pericardium channel point #9 located in the center tip of middle finger.

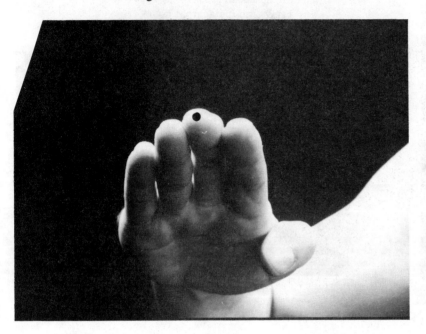

6. Special point on the thumbnail: press on the white half moon shaped area on the thumbnail.

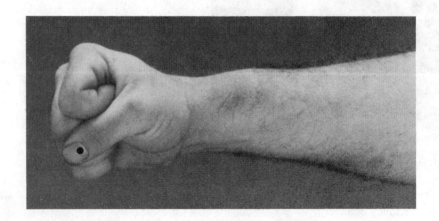

II. THE TRADITIONAL ACUPUNCTURE POINTS USED IN RELAXATION

The following points are commonly used to relax, rejuvenate, and strengthen one's body and mind in Traditional Oriental Medicine. These points can be used before and after training or competition to relieve tension and stress placed on one's body and mind. Some of these points are the same as in the first aid treatments.

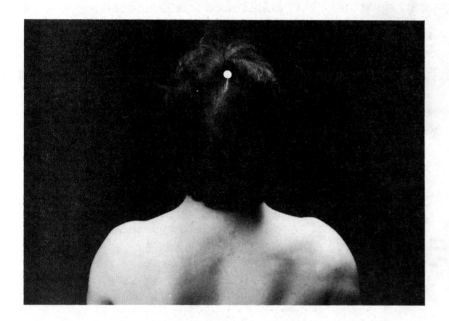

HEAD REGION:

1. GV-20:
Governing channel point #20 located on the top of head on the midpoint of a line connecting tips of both ears. This point will calm the mind and relieve headache and dizziness.

2. Yintang
located on midpoint between two eyebrows. This point will calm the mind and relieve headache and dizziness (same as GV-20).

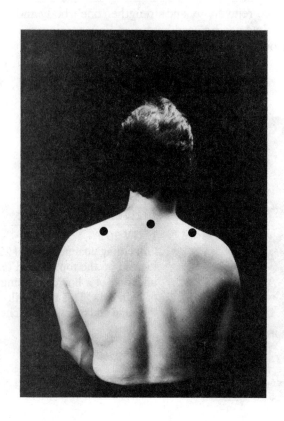

NECK REGION:

1. GV-14:
Governing channel point #14 located between the spinous process of the 7th cervical vertebrae and 1st thoracic vertebrae. This point will calm the mind.

2. GB-21:
Gall Bladder channel point #21 located on shoulder ½ way between lower border of 7th cervical vertebrae and acromion. This point will relieve tension built around the shoulder area.

HAND REGION:

1. LI-4:
this is the same point as used on first aid. Pressing this point will relieve fatigue and relax all the muscles in the body. In addition, it will relieve headache in front part of the head.

3. P-6:
Pericardium channel point #6 located on the medical side of the forearm, 3 finger width above the center of wrist crease between two tendons (palmaris longus & flexor carpi radialis). This point will calm the mind and help stop pain. It will also relieve migraine headache.

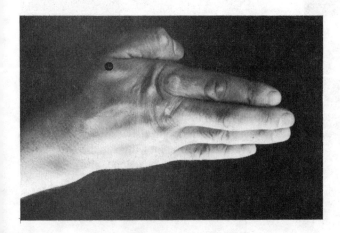

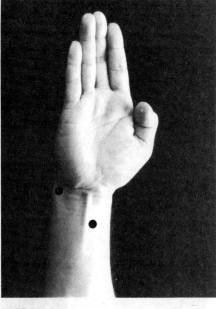

2. H-7:
Heart channel point #7 located on the wrist. With palm up, locate the point at transverse crease of the wrist medial to the tendon of flexor carpi ulnaris. This point has calming action on the heart and mind.

4. SI-3:
Small Intestine channel point #3 located lateral and posterior to head of 5th metacarpal bone at the end of the transverse crease with hand clenched into fist. This point will calm the mind and relax all the muscles in the body.

LEG REGION:

1. ST-36:
This is the same point as used for first aid. Traditionally, this point has been used for longevity, and pressing this point will relieve fatigue and relax all the muscles in the body. In addition, this point will strengthen all the muscles and help the digestion and elimination.

2. GB-34:
Gall Bladder channel point #34 located on the lower leg in the hollow anterior and inferior to the head of the fibula. This is an influential point, and it can relax and/or strengthen all the tendons in the body.

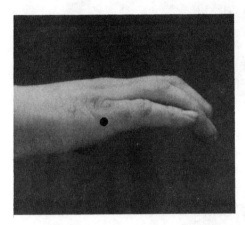

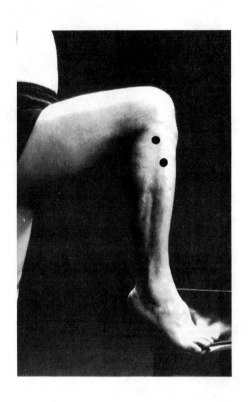

FOOT REGION:

1. LIV-3:
Liver channel point #3 located on the foot about 1.5 inch above web between 1st and 2nd toes. This point has a calming action on the whole body and will relieve "top of the head". Headaches.

2. UB-60:
Urinary Bladder channel point #60 located in the depression ½ way between lateral malleolus and the Achilles' tendon. This is one of the most commonly used points for relieving pain, especially due to injury. It will relax the muscles and tendons in the body. It can also strengthen the lower back and remove headaches at the back of the head.

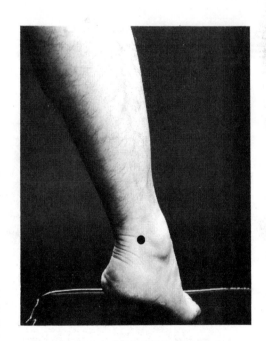

1985 Los Angeles "OPEN" Martial Arts Championship.

Mr. Rick Kenton in action at the 1985 Los Angeles "OPEN".

Tony "Satch" Williams, Grand Champion of the 1986 Los Angeles "OPEN".

Mr. Rick Kenton in action at the 1985 Los Angeles "OPEN".

T.A.G.B. Chairman Bob Howe with Master Cho at the 1986 English Championships.

Welcome address from Master Cho at the 1988 World Championships in England.

Entrance of the U.S. Team at the 1988 World T.K.D. Championships, England.

Mr. George Chueng with Master Cho.

T.A.G.B. Vice Chairman Michael Dew.

T.A.G.B. Chairman David Oliver with Kenny Walton.

Master Cho with attendees after a 1984 T.A.G.B. seminar in Western England.

Master Cho signing autographs at the World Championships in England, 1988.

Entrance of the members of the United States Team at the World Championships in England, 1988.

1985 Scottish Championship Winners.

A.I.T.K.D. members after a December, 1988 seminar taught by Master Cho.

From left to right: Master Bong Soo Han, Mr. Chuck Norris, Master Hee Il Cho and Mr. Bob Wall at Las Vegas, 1988.

T.A.G.B. members after a seminar taught by Master Cho in December, 1988.

Master Cho with some of his Black Belt students.

Master Cho conducting a Black Belt class at the AIMAA World Headquarters in Los Angeles, California.

Master Cho conducting a seminar in Ireland, 1984.

Shown with Master Cho are Mr. Branden O'Toole, Ms. Ann Slocum and Mr. Adrian Walsh in Ireland, 1985.

Dear Martial Artists,

It is with great pleasure that I invite you to join the Action International Martial Arts Association. AIMAA is an international organization which I founded in 1982 to serve as a unifying body for all different styles of the martial arts. The AIMAA charter is devoted to the concept of peace and harmony brought about through an understanding of all types martial arts.

If you choose to become affiliated with the AIMAA you would be making a very sincere statement about what you believe the martial arts to be all about. Additionally, if you are an instructor and your school teaches Tae Kwon Do, you will be able to have your students belt levels certified by myself with grade certificates being issued directly from the World Headquarters in Los Angeles. Since its inception, AIMAA has had thousands of people swell its membership ranks, with dozens of affiliated schools all over the world.

The benefits for an individual school are as follows:
- A signed SCHOOL CHARTER.
- INSTRUCTOR CERTIFICATIONS.
- QUARTERLY AIMAA NEWSLETTER.
- STUDENT INTERNATIONAL RANK RECOGNITION. (These will be approved and provided by AIMAA from your own school's testing results up to the 1st degree black belt level. Official AIMAA rank will be given to all Korean stylists holding a black belt certificate including International Tae Kwon Do, World Tae Kwon Do, Tank Soo Do, Mu Duck Kwon and others. Other fighting arts will be granted all AIMAA privileges except for rank recognition. Any martial artist willing to learn a Korean system will receive an official AIMAA rank.)
- DELUXE INSTRUCTOR'S KIT.
- VOLUME DISCOUNTS ON ALL AIMAA BOOKS AND VIDEO TAPES.

All students of an AIMAA affiliated school who have joined the Association receive additional benefits:

- TRAINING FOR TEN DAYS ANYWHERE IN THE WORLD, AT ANY AIMAA AFFILIATED SCHOOL.
- A 25% DISCOUNT ON ALL AIMAA PRODUCTS, BOOKS AND VIDEO TAPES (Non-Sale items).
- QUARTERLY NEWSLETTER.
- MEMBERSHIP CARD AND AIMAA FRONT PATCH.
- REGISTRATION DISCOUNT FOR ALL BLACK BELT JUDGES at AIMAA sanctioned tournaments.

It is our aim to promote goodwill amongst all martial artists; to teach that it is peace, harmony and truth that are the guides to universal happiness. These basic, fundamental elements are found in the teachings of all systems of martial arts. By being aware of what we have to give, together we can help to create a less violent, more understanding world.

Sincerely,

MASTER HEE IL CHO
President, AIMAA

For Further information, please don't hesitate to contact Master Cho at the following address:

MASTER HEE IL CHO
AIMAA WORLD HEADQUARTERS
11304 1/2 Pico Blvd.
Los Angeles, CA 90064
(213) 477-4067

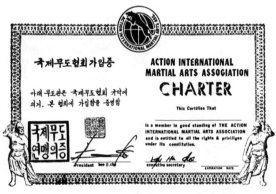

MASTER HEE IL CHO, 8TH BLACK BELT AND PRESIDENT OF AIMAA CHIEF INSTRUCTOR OF THE 10,000 MEMBER, T.A.G.B. AND A.I.T.A. ASSO.

MASTER HEE IL CHO Presents THE COMPLETE MARTIAL ARTISTS
VIDEO LIBRARY
"SEE WHAT'S MISSING IN YOUR TRAINING"

For almost forty years, one of the most influential voices in the martial arts has belonged to Master Hee Il Cho. In addition to being an Eighth Degree Belt in Tae Kwon Do, author of 11 books, and creator of the most extensive video training program in the world (over 30 tapes), Master Cho is recognized as one of the most innovative martial artists alive. An inductee into the Hall of Fame, Master Cho continues to train and refine the martial arts, passing his knowledge on to students in over twenty countries.

Tapes:
1. TAE KWON DO BASIC TECHNIQUES AND STANCES — 60 min
2. THE COMPLETE STRETCH — 60 min
3. ONE STEP AND THREE STEP SPARRING — 60 min
4. TAE KWON DO HYUNG (1-10) — 60 min
5. TAE KWON DO HYUNG (11-20) — 90 min
6. DYNAMIC KICKING - COMPLETE — 80 min
7. DYNAMIC JUMP KICK - COMPLETE — 90 min
8. MASTER CHO'S UNIQUE WORKOUT SYSTEM — 60 min
9. DYNAMIC BREAKING - COMPLETE — 90 min
10. SELF DEFENCE AND FALLING — 120 min
11. FREE SPARRING - AMATEUR TAE KWON DO & AMERICAN ONE POINT — 90 min
12. FREE SPARRING - PROFESSIONAL FULL CONTACT — 60 min
13. DYNAMIC BAG WORKOUT - COMPLETE — 60 min
14. INSTRUCTOR TRAINING - THE COMPLETE ADULT'S CLASS — 60 min
15. INSTRUCTOR TRAINING - THE COMPLETE CHILDREN'S CLASS — 60 min
16. DYNAMIC WEIGHT LIFTING - COMPLETE — 120 min
17. COMPLETE TESTING GUIDE - WHITE THROUGH 3rd DAN BLACK — 120 min
18-VOL.1 HIGHLIGHTS OF THE EIGHTH ANNUAL L.A. OPEN CHAMPIONSHIP — 60 min
18-VOL.II HIGHLIGHTS OF THE EIGHTH ANNUAL L.A. OPEN CHAMPIONSHIP — 60 min
19. HIGHLIGHTS OF THE 18 TAPES — 60 min
20. BOXING (BEGINNERS & ADVANCED) — 80 min
21. ADULTS DEFENCE WORKOUT — 60 min
22. ADULTS SELF DEFENCE — 60 min
23 A. HIGHLIGHTS OF THE TENTH ANNUAL L.A. OPEN CHAMPIONSHIPS — 60 min
23 B. HIGHLIGHTS OF THE TENTH ANNUAL L.A. OPEN CHAMPIONSHIPS — 60 min
24. THE COMPLETE TAE GEUK HYUNG NO. 1 to NO. 8 & KO-RYO — 60 min
25. CHILDREN'S MARTIAL ARTS TRAINING BEGINNERS — 60 min
26. CHILDREN'S MARTIAL ARTS TRAINING - INTERMEDIATE — 60 min
27. CHILDREN'S MARTIAL ARTS TRAINING - ADVANCED — 60 min
28. CHILDREN'S MARTIAL ARTS TRAINING - SELF DEFENCE — 60 min
29. CHILDREN'S MARTIAL ARTS TRAINING - SPARRING AND BREAKING — 60 min
30. HIGHLIGHTS OF THE 20 to 29 — 60 min
31. THE COMPLETE BLACK BELT HYUNG (WTF) — 60 min

ACTION POSTER COLLECTION

A) 22½" × 18". $6.00
B) 22½" × 18". $6.00
C) 22½" × 18". $6.00
D) 22½" × 18". $6.00
E) 24" × 34". $10.00
F) 24" × 34". $10.00

SYBERVISION - Defend Yourself! $89.95

The Sybervision Corp. selected Master Cho from all the instructors nationwide as the perfect model for this self defense program designed for martial artists and non-students alike.

◄ **MASTER CHO'S ACTION POSTERS**
Captured at full power and in beautiful color, these are a handsome addition to the collections of any martial artist. Poster prices include shipping.

NAME _____
ADDRESS _____
CITY _____ STATE _____ ZIP _____
COUNTRY _____

SHIPPING FEE IS $5.00 EACH ADDITIONAL TAPE ADD. $1.50 NO C.O.D.
FOREIGN COUNTRY $10.00 EACH ADDITIONAL TAPE ADD. $7.00
MAKE CHECK PAYABLE TO CHO'S TAEKWONDO CENTER
11304 ½ Pico Blvd., Los Angeles, CA 90064 ● (213) 477-4067
CALIFORNIA RESIDENTS 6½ TAX ● CATALOG (45 PGS) $2.00

REG. EACH TAPES $85.00
ONE TAPE $59.00
ANY OF TWO TAPES $80.00
FOUR TAPES $150.00
(Not including shipping fee)

VISA, MASTER CHARGE ACCEPTED
PAY IN U.S. DOLLARS ONLY (213) 477-4067
CARD NO. _____
EXPIRATION DATE _____
SIGNATURE _____ PHONE _____

TAPE	1	2	3	4	5	6	7	8	9	10	11	12	13	14	15	16
QNTY																

TAPE	17	18-1	18-2	19	20	21	22	23A	23B	24	25	26	27	28	29	30	31
QNTY																	

☐ VHS ☐ BETA ☐ NTSC (USA) ☐ PAL (EUROPE)
(SYSTEM) (FORMAT)

TAPE 1 - Tae Kwon Do Basic Techniques and Stances
Follow a step-by-step in-depth demonstration in slow-motion and full speed of all basic and advanced techniques and stances.

TAPE 2 - The Complete Stretch
Become one of those artists you've admired who are capable of throwing kicks high and hard. This tape leads you through Master Cho's proven stretching techniques by isolating and working each particular muscle group.

TAPE 3 - One Step & Three Step Sparring
Learn essential preparation for free-fighting activities. Develop rapid and accurate combinations of blocking and counter attacking techniques against your opponents.

TAPE 4 - Tae Kwon Do Hyung (1 - 10)
Detailed explanation of techniques, stances and movements in slow-motion and full-speed. Chun Ji, Dan Gun, Do San, Won Hyo, Yul Kok, Joong Gun, Toi Gye, Haw Rang, Choong Moo, Gwang Gae.

TAPE 5 - Tae Kwon Do Hyung (11 - 20)
Detailed explanation of techniques, stances and movements in slow-motion and full-speed. Ge Back, Po Eun, Choong Jang, Ul ji, Yoo Sin, Ko Dong, Choi Youn, Sam Il, Se Jong, Tong Il

TAPE 6 - Dynamic Kicking - Complete !
Follow step-by-step through 9 series of kicking techniques, Each exercise and kick is demonstrated and explained for your individual workout.

TAPE 7 - Dynamic Jump Kick - Complete !
Follow step-by-step through a series of jumping techniques. Each exercise and jumping kick is demonstrated and explained for your individual workout.

TAPE 8 - Master Cho's Unique Workout System
Follow Master Cho step-by-step through a series of full-body exercises. Proper use of weight training, bag workout, boxing techniques and other necessary exercises for the development of the complete martial artist.

TAPE 9 - Dynamic Breaking - Complete !
Improve your speed, power and precision with step-by-step illustrations which guide you through a progressive training program in breaking techniques. Filmed at 500 frames per second.

TAPE 10 - Self Defense & Falling
Learn how to fall and select good defensive stances incorporating hand positions that minimize target areas accessible to the opponent. All techniques are explained and demonstrated.

TAPE 11 - Free Sparring - Amateur
Amateur Tae Kwon Do and American One Point sparring. Develop winning techniques and strategies for point fighting. Master Cho teaches you in slow motion and full-speed.

TAPE 12 - Free Sparring - Professional Full Contact
The skills of a martial artist with the stamina of a boxer. If this sounds like something you wish to achieve, then this tape is it. Develop full contact fighting skills. Learn effective boxing techniques to include in your martial arts training.

TAPE 13 - Dynamic Bag Workout - Complete !
Follow step-by-step through a series of special bag workouts to develop hand speed and punching ability as well as powerful kicks including counter attacks and jumping kicks.

TAPE 14 - Instructor - The Complete Adult Class
Follow Master Cho step-by-step through a series of training exercises for adult students. Learn how to teach and motivate your students, and develop their self-awareness and self-confidence.

TAPE 15 - Instructor - The Complete Children's Class
Follow Master Cho step-by-step through a series of training exercises for young students. Learn how to control and inspire, children and develop their character through the martial arts.

TAPE 16 - Dynamic Weight Lifting - Complete !
Follow Master Cho step-by-step through a series of 30 years of experience-proven weight training workouts. Learn how to build muscle groups for effective and faster techniques and explosive power.

TAPE 17 - Complete Testing Guide
White to high Black Belt Promotions. In this unique guide to promotions, Master Cho covers both the physical as well as the philosophical aspects of a belt test.

TAPE 18 - Eighth Annual L.A. Open Championship VOL. 1
TAPE 18 - Eighth Annual L.A. Open Championship VOL. 2
TAPE 19 - Highlights of The 18 Tapes
TAPE 20 - TAPE 20 - Boxing (Beginners & Advanced)
Dalailed explanation of techniques, stances and movements in slow-motion and full-speed.

TAPE 21 - Adult's Defense Workout
A complete martial arts workout for the non-martial artist including Flexability Training, Endurance Training, Cardiovascular and Muscular Conditioning as well as the most practical of MASTER CHO'S moves to both condition as well as to develop your own personal Defense System.

TAPE 22 - Adult's Self Defense
A sensible system of self defense for both the martial artist as well as the non-martial artist. MASTER CHO covers how to escape from an attacker's grasp, how to control an attacker through the use of joint locking techniques, and when necessary, how to take away an attacker's ability to cause further harm through a devastating counter attack.

TAPE 23A - Tenth Annual L.A. Open Championships
All the action from the Tenth Annual Los Angeles OPEN Martial Arts Championships, held on May 17, 1987 in Beverly Hills and hosted by MASTER HEE IL CHO. Edited from over eight hours of non-stop action, included are junior and adult sparring, black belt sparring, Grand Champion match and more.

TAPE 23B - The Tenth Annual L.A. Open Championships
This second volume includes forms competition, women's sparring, master's demonstrations and more.

TAPE 24 - The Complete Tae Geuk Hyung 1 to 8 - & Koryo
MASTER HEE IL CHO teaches and demonstrates and new patterns as sanctioned by the World Tae Kwon Do Federation (WTF), from White belt through 1st Dan Black belt. Tae Geuk 1-8 as well as the Koryo pattern are shown at different speeds and different angles to make learning as easy as possible.

TAPE 25 - Children's Martial Arts Training, Beginners
All the basics that the younger martial artist needs to begin his or her training including Meditation, Warm-up Exercises and Stretching, Basic Stances, Blocks, Attacking Techniques and Kicks.

TAPE 26 - Children's Martial Arts Training, Intermediate
Children's intermediate techniques are explained in a follow along fashion, including combinations of Blocks, Block/Punch Techniques, Fighting Techniques and Intermediate Kicking Techniques as well as Stick Exercises to help develop balance.

TAPE 27 - Children's Martial Arts Training, Advanced
A young person's guide to advanced techniques. Covered in detail are intricate Hand Techniques, Advanced Kicking and Kicking Combination Techniques, and how to train using a variety of hand held targets.

TAPE 28 - Children's Martial Arts Training, Self-Defense
Unfortunately, a must in today's world. Children's Self-Defense training is covered in detail including how to attempt to escape from Bear Hugs, Wrist Grabs, Shoulder Grabs, Head Locks and other restraining holds, as well as what to do once free. How and when Children should defend themselves is also discussed.

TAPE 29 - Children's Martial Arts Training, Sparring & Breaking
Children's Sparring and Demonstrations, including Arrangement Sparring, Free Sparring, working out using a hanging bag, and a demonstration of children's Jumping and Board Breaking Techniques.

TAPE 30 - Highlights of Tapes 20 to 29

TAPE 31 - THE COMPLETE TAEKWONDO HYUNG (WTF)
Geum-Gahg, Tae-Baek, Pyeong-Won, Sip-Jin, Ji Tae, Cheon-Kwon, Han-Soo, Il-Yeo. MASTER HEE IL CHO teaches and demonstrates and new patterns, as sanctioned by the world Tae Kwon Do Federation (WTF), from 2nd Dan to 9th black belt pattern are shown dat different speeds and different angles to make learning as easy as possible.

Master Hee Il Cho - Early Years of Competition

Master Hee Il Cho - Early Years of Competition

Scene from "The Best of the Best"

In 1989, Master Cho was asked to portray the coach of the Korean martial arts Team in the movie "The Best of the Best." Eric Roberts stars as a member of the American team and James Earl Jones plays his coach. This movie is about the bond that forms between people and will touch your heart. The competition scenes include some of the most dynamic kicking techniques ever captured on film, and it is this type of movie which portrays the "right" image of the martial arts that will help all students, regardless of system or style.

"The Best of the Best" is scheduled to open in the Winter of 1989, and Master Cho would like to see the entire martial arts community support the film.

Master Cho and world famous actor James Earl Jones. Actor and teacher Simon Rhee with his father,

Actor Eric Roberts with Master Cho.

Master Cho, film producer and actor Philip Rhee, and Eric Roberts.

Actor Christopher Penn with Master Cho.

Master Cho with members of the "Korean Team"

Scene from "The Best of the Best"

Korean Special Forces Unit with Master Cho,

Simon Rhee and Philip Rhee.

Location filming in the snow and cold in Korea.

James Earl Jones as the American Coach with Master Cho and Sally Kirkland